mindful as f*ck

100 Simple Exercises
TO LET THAT SH*T GO!

Emily Horn

ADAMS MEDIA
New York London Toronto Sydney New Delhi

Adams media

Adams Media
An Imprint of Simon & Schuster, Inc.
100 Technology Center Drive
Stoughton, MA 02072

First Adams Media hardcover edition October 2020

ADAMS MEDIA and colophon are trademarks of Simon & Schuster.

For information about special discounts for bulk purchases, please contact Simon & Schuster Special Sales at 1-866-506-1949 or business@simonandschuster.com.

The Simon & Schuster Speakers Bureau can bring authors to your live event. For more information or to book an event contact the Simon & Schuster Speakers Bureau at 1-866-248-3049 or visit our website at www.simonspeakers.com.

Interior design by Priscilla Yuen
Interior illustrations by Eric Andrews and Priscilla Yuen
Interior images © Getty Images/ Color_Brush

Manufactured in the United States of America

3 2021

Library of Congress Cataloging-in-Publication Data has been applied for.

ISBN 978-1-5072-1425-1
ISBN 978-1-5072-1426-8 (ebook)

contents

introduction

If you sleep through yoga, hate the taste of green juice, and have never said a mantra with a straight face, *Mindful As F*ck* is here for you!

This book has one hundred simple exercises for embracing mindfulness in a way that works for you. (And that way is easy and entertaining.) You'll find lessons and learnings on everything from how to actually sit still with your thoughts to finally figuring out just what a chakra is to setting an intention that you'll actually follow. It's the perfect way to embrace mindfulness—without losing your mind.

So if you're stressed out, *Mindful As F*ck* is just the friend you need. With this book by your side you'll always remember to take a deep breath, stand up straight, and let that sh*t go.

what is all this stuff?

The world is stressful, and what makes it worse is that there are just too many goddamn ways to relax. Some of these are expensive, some are confusing, and some are just dumb. (Ever heard of yoni eggs? *Shudder*.) Luckily, there are a few ways to break through the noise of the world and pursue a more aligned life with minimal embarrassment and only a little bullshit.

It turns out you don't need to abandon everything you know about breathing or start adding essential oils to everything in order to get in touch with a more mindful life. Mindful living happens one step at a time, so cut yourself a break and start slowly.

The exercises in this book are fun-sized by design, and like most fun-sized things, you can either enjoy them all at once or save them for when you really need a treat. Think of them as building blocks for an eventual routine, instead of as a hundred things you must do right at this moment or else be sent to a mindfulness prison staffed by people with amazing abs taking a break from their beachfront acro-yoga sessions. For the most part, these exercises won't rearrange your day or even require you to put on pants. All you have to do is chill the fuck out.

Mindfulness didn't just materialize out of the air as a way to sell expensive moisture-wicking leggings and candles that smell like a barnyard. Mindfulness is popular because our world of constant stimulation makes it easy to disconnect from who we are on the most basic level. And quite frankly, that sucks.

Living with intention and all that shit is a way to maintain a healthy sense of self and sanity in a world that moves NASCAR fast. There are tons of different ways to go about this, so let's dive in! In this book, we're going to draw on seven unique disciplines:

1. Meditation
2. Yoga
3. Buddhism
4. Ayurveda
5. Reiki
6. Chakra healing
7. The Law of Attraction

Let's break them down one at a time.

Meditation

Meditation sounds so simple on paper—you sit down, think about nothing, and voila! Enlightenment. But in practice, it's a totally different story. It feels like the second you sit down every force in the universe conspires against you—you can't get comfortable, there's an annoying buzzing sound coming from your lamp, or you're just so tired you fall asleep. Meditation is fucking *hard*.

Part of what makes meditation feel so challenging is that there's a ton of bullshit surrounding it that makes it seem especially hard to even get started. For instance, if you think that meditation requires you to sit alone for hours on a mountaintop with no other obligation other than to seek enlightenment, then yeah, that shit is going to feel impossible. The reality is that you can meditate anywhere—those spare five minutes between meetings, waiting in line for your cappuccino, that time before bed while you're waiting to fall asleep and thinking about how you probably should have meditated.

You're going to notice that some words crop up over and over again when talking meditation. Here's a quick glossary so you can wise up and get to chillin'.

- **Awareness:** Awareness is how you go from numbing out to tuning in. It's all about turning on your five senses to really engage with the world around you.

- **Contemplation:** Contemplation is all about using your senses to learn something new through total immersion. It's going to involve a lot of creepy staring and stoner-in-philosophy-class-style revelations.

- **Focus:** Paying attention, but like *super attention*.

- **Visualization:** Using your mind to create images— for instance, there may not be an existing memory of you nailing every word to "Baby Got Back" at karaoke, but through visualization, anything is possible.

Yoga

You've probably at least *tried* yoga by now. Unfortunately, you've also probably hated it. Your mat smells like sweat, the person next to you is effortlessly putting her foot behind her head, and the instructor is always telling you to breathe and you're just like, "What does it look like I'm doing?" All these things make it very, very easy to turn against yoga. But yoga, despite its challenges, really fucking works.

One of the best things you can do is to approach yoga with an open mind. Yoga is an ancient practice, so don't let modern bullshit get in the way of your enjoyment of it. For centuries people have benefitted from yoga, using movement to connect the mind, body, and spirit into one kick-ass machine. Yoga is not about paying $40 a class to be told what to do by someone named "Rainstorm." It's about joining parts of yourself together and enjoying the challenge.

It's also easy to hate on yoga if you're not naturally flexible or athletic, but yoga isn't something only double-jointed cheerleader types can do. Remember, the foundation of yoga isn't flexibility or strength; it's posture and breath work, and no matter what shape you're in, you possess these resources. There are also a few other items that might be helpful to have:

- **Nonslip mat:** Yoga is all about knowing yourself, so be honest with yourself that sometimes even the most graceful yogis fall over and hit their heads on the dresser. Get a mat with some traction to minimize trouble.

- **Strap or belt:** A versatile tool that can be used to stretch your hamstrings, help you open up certain stretches, and pretend to be more flexible than you are.

- **Metal or wooden chair without arms:** A chair is wonderful for supported and modified poses. Just don't use it for regular sitting down.

- **Wooden or foam block:** If you can touch your toes you may not need this, but if you can't (no shame here), this helps "bring the floor to you." You could also use a phone book if those still exist, or the LSAT prep book you bought when you thought that was a thing that might happen.

- **Empty wall space:** A plain old wall is one of the best ways to correct your posture and keep you standing straight.

Buddhism

While Buddhism can be a personal religious identity, it can also be something you *do* rather than something you are. To practice Buddhism you don't need to call yourself a Buddhist; you just need to sit your ass down and get to meditating.

Buddhism goes back to the Buddha (shocker!), a yogi who lived more than 2,500 years ago in northern India. The Buddha's most notable teaching is that "life is suffering." Cheery, right? He was onto something—in the Buddha's mind, desire was the root of suffering, and suffering throughout the world was nurtured by desire and its bedfellows of greed and delusion.

Maybe you, too, have found yourself on the hamster wheel of desire and suffering. Consider the last time you wanted something. Now think about what happened when you got it. How quickly did the next desire set in? How quickly did what you have become not enough? Exactly. The goal is to end this suffering by cutting off desire at the root, and achieve a state known as "Nirvana."

So how exactly do we just shut off the faucet of wanting to buy new shit? It's as simple as breathing and sitting. Yes, the thing you are probably doing right at this very moment (unless you're one of those standing desk weirdos) can be harnessed for your own inner peace.

Get Your Breath Together

You breathe all the time without thinking of it, which is actually kind of amazing. You're so fucking boss at the thing your body needs to stay alive that you do it without even thinking of it!

Don't stay on your high horse too long. Practice a few different kinds of breaths and get used to how they feel. Breathe in your nose and out your mouth. Try to draw a breath from your diaphragm and really feel the different parts of your body expand. Get in touch with your natural breath and get to know its rhythm. The simplest way to do this is by counting. Breathe in, breathe out, and count "one." Keep going until you hit ten and try not to let your mind wander. Mindful breathing takes practice, but it will help your mind be quiet eventually.

Sitters Aren't Quitters

It turns out that sitting can be just as complicated as breathing, which is frustrating since these two things are kind of Buddhism's whole deal. There are very few Buddhism-influenced exercises in this book that don't begin with sitting, so find a way that works for you. Maybe lotus, otherwise known as "crisscross applesauce," is perfect for you, or maybe it helps to have a cushion supporting your back or butt. You want to straddle the line of comfort—if anything is off, you'll fidget and have trouble focusing, but if you're too comfy you'll find yourself taking a ton of unplanned naps.

Ayurveda

There are plenty of great things about modern, Western medicine, from the polio vaccine to whatever the hell it is that Botox does, but that doesn't mean that other, more traditional systems don't have anything to offer. Ayurveda is one of these systems, a holistic view of health that originated in India over five thousand years ago and has been in use ever since.

From acne to stomach trouble to fertility issues, the teachings from Ayurveda can make a solid supplement to current medical wisdom. Most of the appeal of Ayurveda comes from the fact that it's truly holistic, meaning that it treats the person as, well, a whole person.

Doshas: Why You Feel Like That All the Time

The foundation of Ayurveda are the three doshas, which are the dominant elements within the body. There are three types of doshas: vata, pitta, and kapha. And while all three exist to some degree in each person, they vary in how dominant they are. Vata features the ether and air elements, kapha is water and earth, and pitta combines fire and water.

Ayurveda dictates that your dosha was set in a specific pattern while you were in utero, and then the second you came to Earth, external forces have been fucking up your internal ratios ever since. Perfect health in Ayurveda means returning to this original balance, so the first step when embarking on an Ayurvedic journey is figuring out just what your constitution is and what the fuck it takes to bring that harmony back. Use the following lists as a starting point for understanding your current ratios of vata, pitta, and kapha—since your ratios can change by the day, these are more of a jumping-off point than a diagnostic tool.

hello mother, hello vata:

- Do you talk quickly and often to the point where sometimes you realize even *you* don't know what the fuck is going on anymore?

- Do you often feel anxious even when you aren't reading about volcanoes that are overdue to explode by thousands of years?

- Are you constipated? Don't be embarrassed; poop comes up *a lot* in Ayurveda.

- Are you more comfortable seeing the big picture rather than the small details?

- Do you find it easy to believe in concepts other people might find a little silly, perhaps, oh, I don't know, Ayurveda?

These questions can help you see if vata is particularly present in your body. Talking quickly and constantly? That's mobile vata at work. Constipation? One word: dry. An affinity for cosmic and spiritual concepts? That just means the subtle and ethereal qualities of vata are hard at work in you.

throw a pitta party:

- Are you able to efficiently complete tasks with the single-mindedness of a trained assassin?

- Do you have a short fuse that can be set off by anything from systemic injustice to someone breathing too loudly?

- Are you highly critical of yourself, to the point where if you heard someone talk about your mom the way you talk about yourself, you'd challenge that person to pistols at dawn?

- Are you usually hot, even when everyone else is wrapped in twenty different shawls in an attempt to fight off the office AC?

- Do you argue mostly by saying, "Well, that's your opinion," even when you know someone is telling you literal facts?

If you answered "yes" to any of those questions, consider you might have some pitta at play within you, even if it isn't dominant. For instance, anger, overheating, and a short temper align with the fiery and mobile qualities of pitta.

kapha the mornin' to ya:

- Do you gain weight easily and have difficulty losing it? Ugh, bodies, right?

- Is it hard to find the motivation to get up and go, even if you're already behind schedule because you hit the snooze button roughly four hundred times (give or take)?

- Are you prone to depression or even just defeatism?

- Do you sleep like a fucking brick?

- Are you loyal to your friends and family? Do you believe that snitches get stitches?

These traits all correspond to kapha, a grounded, gross (as opposed to "subtle") dosha. Because of its ties to the earth element, kapha tends to be steady and solid, which explains the persistent desire to sleep the day away. An uncharitable reading of kapha qualities might see kapha-dominant people as lazy, but the steadiness and stillness of kapha that this dosha is a calming and nurturing presence.

Ideally, you should be able to check a few things off each list. All of these doshas exist somewhere in you, and it's up to you to find a balance that works.

Reiki

If you've ever looked into Reiki before, you may still have some lingering questions. Like, What the fuck? Is Reiki a physical feeling? A religion? A medical treatment? Part of a spa day?

Not to confuse you more, but Reiki is somehow all of these things. Some people use it for physical wellness while other people use it to relax. Some people infuse their own beliefs about the nature of the universe into their Reiki routine while others keep their faith and Reiki practice separate. This is all great news for you, because there are a million and one ways to understand Reiki, and there are just as many ways to apply it to your life.

Universal What Now?

The word "Reiki" is a combination of two Japanese syllables, *rei* and *ki* (pronounced "ray key"), which translates to "universal life energy." What the fuck is that? Drawn from the concept of "ki" (which you may have seen spelled in other places as chi or qi), it's the idea that there isn't just a life force sustaining us as individuals, but also one we share with the entire living world. This force is in everyone and everything, from your neighbor's dog to your friend's niece. Reiki doesn't just refer to this energy, but also to the practices that move it around, so you can move Reiki by doing Reiki, or do Reiki because you have some Reiki that needs to be moved.

How Does Reiki Do the Thing?

While Reiki is thought to enter the body through your various chakras (more on this later), there are all kinds of shit that can get in its way. Reiki can become overly concentrated in certain areas or blocked from flowing to others, and it's up to you to use your intuition to smooth things out.

Sure, all this stuff about ki and energy transfer sounds dope, but how do you get started doing it for yourself? It all begins with a gentle touch, aka your etheric hand. Yes, the moment you lay your hands on your body to start a Reiki treatment, your hands get an upgrade from "regular" to "goddamn magical." Just about every Reiki treatment uses the palms as the focal point for energy transfer. You don't want to apply pressure, but just rest your hands gently upon your body.

Reiki is as much physical as it is emotional, so if you don't know where to start treatments, don't be afraid to go with the obvious. If you get frequent tension headaches, start at your temples. If you struggle with voicing your true feelings, maybe your diaphragm and throat need some energy unblocked. The more you get in touch with yourself, the more effective Reiki can be.

Is There Any Way to Know It's Working?

The problem with channeling an invisible and omnipresent force is that you're never really sure if you have a hold on it or not. It's okay to be skeptical and join the crowd of people who use Reiki purely for relaxation. People tend to report having the most success when doing treatments in solitude, either in quiet or with chill music being played in the background. As long as you can carve out some time to really focus, even if it's just five minutes, you'll get an A for effort.

Chakra Healing

Don't get freaked out by this, but you have *seven* chakras chilling in your body *right now*. So what the fuck are chakras? Primarily, they're energy centers—points on your body where your life force, energy, and *je ne sais quoi* are most concentrated and where that universal energy you learned about in the Reiki section can really flow. Some people visualize them as little orbs of spinning light, while some people just feel them as a spiritual presence. No matter how you choose to vibe with your chakras, a crucial step on the path to mindfulness and generally feeling good is getting in tune with these metaphysical bad boys.

Why Should I Give a Shit about Chakras?

Okay, so chakras are spinning energy centers that blah, blah, blah. But why are these little buggers so important? Because when they're off-balance, shit gets all kind of fucked up. On the other hand, when your chakras are aligned, you're basically unstoppable. You can speak your mind without losing track of what you're saying halfway through. You're confident enough in your relationships to text first. You feel capable of solving problems, not just letting them pile up. Here's the breakdown of all your chakras, where to find them, and just what they need to do their thing.

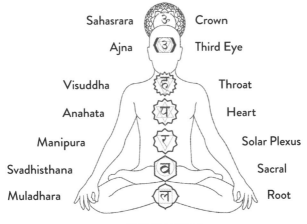

Sahasrara — Crown

Ajna — Third Eye

Visuddha — Throat

Anahata — Heart

Manipura — Solar Plexus

Svadhisthana — Sacral

Muladhara — Root

THE CHAKRAS

Muladhara

The first chakra is called the root chakra, *Muladhara* in Sanskrit. Its location is, shall we say, somewhat indelicate. If you're fancy, it's in your perineum, but if you're the kind of person who laughs at the number 69, it's your taint. If you don't know what either of those things are, it's right between your naughty bits and your pooper.

Don't run away screaming—wellness isn't always *Instagram*-worthy. It might feel weird, but being in touch with this part of your body is a vital way to keep your chakras spinning. This is especially important because the root chakra is thought to hook right into the energy of the earth. Whenever you need to let something go or draw upon some especially powerful energy, this is the chakra to use.

Svadhisthana

To find the location of the second chakra, *Svadhisthana*, otherwise known as the sacral chakra, turn your attention to your lower abdomen, below your belly button. Somewhere, floating between your stomach and lower vertebrae, is chakra number two, which influences the good things in life: creativity, trust, and happiness. This chakra is especially susceptible to bad energy and negativity clogging up the works.

Manipura

Manipura is the name of the third chakra, which is located in the solar plexus region of the body. Its name means "lustrous gem," so it's basically a diamond inside you. If you need help visualizing this chakra's location, place your hand on your front body between your navel and sternum. Inhale so that your body expands into that hand, and as you inhale, really feel the air going into that part of your belly.

Anahata

The fourth chakra, *Anahata*, means "unstruck," also known as your heart chakra. Three guesses as to where it might be located! Breath work and the heart chakra are pretty much best friends, so the more you focus on your breath, the happier Anahata will be.

Vishuddha

The fifth chakra is *Vishuddha*, or the throat chakra, which is the bridge from the heart chakra to the third eye. Located right above the collarbone, it controls your communication. If you feel like you've been suggesting dinner at the Cheesecake Factory for weeks and no one has listened, maybe it's time to give your throat chakra some love. Either that, or find some new friends.

Ajna

The third eye chakra is the most famous chakra and has, without a doubt, the coolest name. Otherwise known as *Ajna*, the third eye is the connection between the craziness of the outside world and the wisdom within you. It's right where you'd imagine a third eye would be on your face: between your eyes and slightly above the brow line.

Sahasrara

Sahasrara is the name of the seventh chakra, aka the crown chakra. Remember how the root chakra connects you to the earth? Well, the crown chakra connects you to everything beyond the earth. It's your link to the energy of the universe and its possibilities, so don't neglect it!

The Law of Attraction

The Law of Attraction has a terrible reputation. Maybe it should! It seems almost too good to be true—you mean you can just *ask* the universe to surround you with puppies and give you the ability to sing like Mariah Carey and suddenly you're belting to an audience of goldendoodles? Sign me up!

Unfortunately, that's not *quite* it. The Law of Attraction is a bit more complex than it seems at first glance. While that can be a bummer for your more outlandish dreams, it can be a real boon to the achievable ones. Sometimes you might feel a little silly or entitled when trying law-of-attraction-based exercises, but asking for what you want has a ton of benefits, from forcing you to drop habits that might get in the way of your success to opening up other people's eyes to ways they might be able to help. Whether you choose to see the Law of Attraction as a vague way to reach your goals or a way to treat cosmic energy like a year-round Santa Claus, plenty of people find parts of its philosophy useful, so pick and choose what works for you!

Like Attracts Like

You've heard people say "birds of a feather flock together," or "ask and ye shall receive." Turns out that clichés have an annoying way of being right, as this is pretty much what the L of A entails. To put it simply, the energy you put out into the world influences the thoughts, people, and circumstances that come into yours.

The most fundamental part of the Law of Attraction is that your thoughts and surroundings matter. For example, if you run with someone who's a bad influence, next thing you know you might find yourself wearing a black leather jacket and having street corner jazz dance battles with rival gangs. Similarly, if you surround yourself with people who lift you up, you'll find yourself somewhere else entirely. Instead of immersing yourself in doubt and denial, go with optimism. Knowingly or unwittingly, we're going to attract whatever it is we think about and experience most. The basic tenet of activating the Law of Attraction is intention, and the more deliberate the intention is, the better.

get ready to manifest the shit out of that intention

1. Manifestation is like the Cha Cha Slide—you need a lot of space in order to do it right. Sweep the mental clutter, confusion, and negativity from your mind. There are tons of ways to do this—breath work, meditation, or journaling are good ways to start. Focus especially on getting the constraints of reality to hit the bricks. Why? Because reality is a party pooper.

2. Once your mind is clear, make a mental declaration of your intent. No maybes or uncertainty. Be bold, be outlandish, and maybe be a little delusional if

you're up for it. Don't talk yourself out of what you want before you've even declared it.

3 Hear yourself out and be open to the idea that maybe, just maybe, your wildest dream is somehow possible. Get excited about the possibilities.

4 Visualize yourself having it. Feel the emotion associated with getting what you want. Reality is going to try and bust in and say all kinds of boring shit like "Aren't most rock climbers not afraid of heights?" or "'Keeper of a haunted lighthouse' hasn't been a viable career path since the 1890s" or "Doesn't Oprah already have a best friend who will probably inherit her fortune?" Don't let it distract you. This is your time.

5 Feel and express gratitude for all the good stuff you already have going. It's easy to get wrapped up in the possibility of some fantastic new life, but the flip side of this is that it will make your current life look extra shitty by comparison. Consider all the things you're grateful for, and take them as proof that the universe has delivered for you already and will do so again.

EXERCISE 1

sit your ass down

We'd all love to sneak away to a mountain or beach and just vibe in search of inner peace, but the world has this tendency to get in the way of that noble goal. The good news is you don't need to travel up a mountain or risk a cabin-in-the-woods situation for the sake of mindfulness—peace is something you can cultivate anytime. The first step is as simple as sitting down.

1 Make sure you're comfy. If you're already wearing sweatpants, put on uglier ones. Wear the big, comfy underwear that you'd never let anyone else see. Drape yourself in enough fabric that you look like an Olsen twin circa 2005.

2 You may associate sitting on the floor with being drunk, but it's also the perfect position for

meditation. Just think, all those nights you've been *mindful* about a *YouTube* video of a fat dog, not *bizarrely distraught* and *killing the mood*.

3 Here's the kick-ass thing about meditation: You call the fucking shots. Close your eyes or open them. Use a wall to support your back if you need it. Go outside! Listen to rain noises! Whatever chills you out is another tool in your arsenal.

4 Okay, here comes the good part: turning off your brain. How? By letting all the bullshit that is weighing you down float to the surface. As it rises up, let it go.

5 If you're struggling to let the outside world go, imagine a place that makes you feel peaceful. A beach without any people, a mountain that somehow still has Wi-Fi, or just a couch you like napping on. There's no wrong answers in meditating. If it calms you down, roll with it.

6 Take a few moments to occupy that space and then, as slowly as you entered it, say goodbye. As you exit, leave all the bullshit you entered with behind.

walking meditation: literally as easy as it sounds

It turns out that a lot of the time we spend strutting around listening to our favorite music doubles as valuable meditation time. Give this a try.

1 Pick a route and get to stepping. It can be around a park or just down your hallway, as long as it's safe and long enough for you to get into a groove.

2 As you walk, let your brain get loud with all the shit that's bothering you. Is it too late to admit I don't know exactly what a Secretary of State does? Does my pet actually think I'm his pet? You know, the big questions.

3 Slow down your steps, and as you change the pace of your feet, change the pace of your thoughts. Repeat a mantra in rhythm with each step. It can be as simple as "I'm grateful" or an Oscar-worthy monologue. Either way, let these words guide you until you reach your destination.

EXERCISE 3
focus up!

If you're putting pressure on yourself to solve the mysteries of the universe while meditating, knock that shit off! It's a one-way ticket to self-doubt. Instead, try a round of single-point meditation, aka focusing intensely on one thing. It's basically obsessing, except instead of thinking of your most embarrassing moments you're thinking of something you love, and it makes you feel better, not worse. Here's how to do it:

1 Choose one thing to concentrate on. Zero in on your breathing, your heartbeat, a color, a sound, a food (definitely a food). The world is full of shitty things, so don't let them intrude.

2 The rest is pretty simple—just stay focused! Whenever you find your focus wandering off, gently remind yourself to return to the original point of concentration. Try to be kind to yourself while you do this—now isn't a good time to call yourself a dumb asshole. Try to hold this focus for a few minutes at first, slowly working your way up to longer intervals.

EXERCISE 4

get aware!

If you're the kind of person who can obsess over one thing already, maybe work on expanding your focus to the bigger picture. Buddhist *vipassana* meditation (literally "special-seeing" or insight meditation) might be the move for you. Try this:

1 Sit in front of something you like looking at, even if it's just a photo of you where you look bomb. Try to avoid messy areas or anything chaotic. This is your field of awareness. Greet it. The two of you are about to get intimate.

2 Now...focus! Take it all in slowly, constantly shifting up your perspective. There's always a new angle to see things from or something you haven't noticed yet waiting to be discovered. Think of yourself as the Christopher Columbus of your field of awareness, without the murder and diseases. Go forth and explore.

3 Whenever some bullshit comes floating into your head from beyond the field of awareness, imagine slapping a sticky note on that bad boy and filing it away for later. This is called "mental noting," and is a great way to keep disruptive thoughts from killing your vibe.

friendly fucking reminder

Mental noting is a nice way to bitch-slap annoying thoughts away without chastising yourself for the distraction. When you note a thought, there's no value judgment about you, just a quick return to the original area of focus.

EXERCISE 5

tell me what you want

(what you really, really want)

Before you dismiss the Law of Attraction outright, try it. There's a ton of reasons to be skeptical, but the whole point of the L of A is that opportunity comes to those with an open mind. Swallow your doubts and get ready to ask the world for what you want.

1. Lie down and clear your mind. If you can't get your head totally clear, at least try to infuse your thoughts with some positivity. It doesn't have to feel inauthentic and cheesy. It's as simple as going from "It's too hot outside today and I hate it" to "Man, it's hot but at least I'm balling out in front of my AC."

2 In the midst of your positive thinking, begin declaring what you want. Make sure to actually DECLARE it—don't be wishy-washy! It might sound crazy to say "I want to be an astronaut" when you don't remember any algebra and hate wearing white, but just saying this desire out loud will move the universe in your direction.

3 Admitting the things we want is scary as hell. Lean into that fear and use it to ask yourself the real shit: "Am I afraid to get what I want?" "What am I afraid would happen if I were to chase it?" Look your fears in their ugly faces and don't back down.

4 Don't ruin this moment with logic! There's a time and place for logic, like the LSATs or picking a karaoke song, but here logic is just another way for you to deny yourself. You know obstacles exist because, quite simply, you aren't stupid. You just don't need to make them bigger than what they already are.

5 The Law of Attraction isn't all about wanting! A major part of the Law of Attraction involves shouting out the things you're already grateful for. Maybe you parallel parked like a boss or finally figured out how to make sourdough. Whatever it is, you deserve some props.

love, even for shitty people

You probably love your mom, your dog, your neighbor's dog, a baby you saw in a video trying a lemon, but those aren't the only worthy targets of all that good energy. All the mindfulness in the world doesn't mean shit unless you direct your love to yourself first. So tell negativity to fuck off, because you're about to fall in love with the face in the mirror.

1 Calm down and clear your mind while sitting or lying somewhere comfortable. This time, though, instead of focusing on a sound or a sight, think of someone you love: Beyoncé! Leonardo! Any drunk woman who has ever given you a compliment! All good choices!

2 Now direct that loving feeling in four ways:

- May you be free from danger; may you be safe. May you never look up and realize everyone in the room with you is in a fraternity and is about to do some kind of handshake that involves chanting.

- May you have happiness; may you have peace. May no one reply to a text just saying "k."

- May you have physical well-being and health. May your knees stop making that clicking noise and may green juice stop tasting like garbage.

- May you have ease of well-being; may you be free from unnecessary struggle and pain. May your inbox always be at zero and the dress code always be "pajama friendly."

3 Direct these feelings toward yourself and let them wash over you.

4 Now that you're full of love, shit is going to get real. Sometimes you have to be the bigger person and apply this thinking to a more difficult person, like a coworker who breathes too loudly. It won't be easy, but practicing love toward your enemies will make you feel more peaceful.

EXERCISE 7
keep on breathing!

Ki is the life force or living energy that connects to all that there is. Everything has ki—trees, rocks, probably some other stuff too! You get it. Long story short, this shit is everywhere, so you better learn how to channel it.

1. Sit upright with your spine straight. Be mindful of your posture—if you slouch like Quasimodo, your ki ain't going to flow.

2. Open your mouth, relax your jaw, stick out your tongue, and pant like a dog. Feel stupid? You're doing it right!

3. Continue for several minutes. These in-and-out breaths, while making you feel like Fido, will open up your belly and clear the ki passageways from the base of your spine to your throat's vocal cords. Once you create a space for your ki to flow cleanly, you'll be able to do whatever you want with it. Go forth and conquer!

EXERCISE 8
get a boost

By now you know that breath work is great for calming you down and inner peace blah, blah, blah—breath goes in, breath goes out, lather, rinse, repeat. If you're getting bored of just breathing and relaxing, try *Kapalabhati Pranayama*, aka "shining skull breathing." This shit is supposed to pump you up and make your face glow like an *Instagram* filter.

1. Sit down and exhale your breath completely.

2. Inhale and then exhale forcefully through your nose. Pretend you're blowing out candles on a cake but with just your nose. Yeah, it's a gross way to describe it. Do it anyway.

3. Repeat! Don't make yourself wheezy or weak, but do it enough times that you feel ready to tackle whatever is facing you, even if it involves feigning enthusiasm about your friend's niece.

stop talking shit

You can say all the affirmations you want, but if you aren't kind to yourself, you're getting in your own way. You don't have to think you're hot shit—let's leave that to the *Instagram* influencers—but treating yourself with kindness is a great step toward getting what you want. Remember all that good shit you wanted back in Exercise 5? The first and most important step is believing that you deserve it. So watch your mouth and talk yourself up.

1. Sit quietly and clear your mind, concentrating on your breathing. Normally meditation is all about clearing your mind, but today you get to mix it the fuck up! Turn your brain on, really paying attention to what it is you're thinking.

2. As thoughts come up, evaluate them! Are they mean? Are they exaggerated? Are they nice? Are they positive? Are they negative? If you notice that you're being a total downer, try to consciously flip

these thoughts in the direction of positivity. You don't have to lie to yourself, because let's face it, sometimes things just fucking suck, but a slight shift in perspective goes a long way. You don't have to use logic or reality to back up your new, positive thoughts. If it makes you feel more positive to simply say, "I'm a superhuman with the power of flight," then that counts! You'll want to get more specific as you go on, but for now, you do you.

3. Remember, positivity takes practice. If it was easy, we'd all walk around acting like elementary school guidance counselors all day. You know, the ones who have puppets to teach you about not smoking? You don't have to get *quite* that peppy, but try spending at least ten minutes a day focusing on reframing negative thoughts. It's the first step to building positivity as a habit.

friendly fucking reminder: fuck off, reality

Sometimes, when you're focusing on yourself and all the great things coming for you, reality has this shitty way of rolling up and messing it up. If your brain is a party of good vibes, reality is the guy no one invited who brought his guitar. Don't let reality make you doubt your own awesomeness, and don't let that guy play "Wonderwall."

take a chill pill

Usually we count on TV, music, and podcasts about serial killers to calm us down, but learning how to relax yourself is a different ballgame. While there are a lot of ways to do it, serious yogis use a pose called *Savasana*, which forces your body and mind to get their shit together.

1 Lie down on your back with your legs extended and put a folded blanket under your head and neck. Comfortable but not too comfortable is the vibe you're going for, like one of those living rooms where all the furniture is wrapped in plastic.

2 Tense up your WHOLE BODY. Yes, everything—arms, legs, shoulders—really get in there. If you're already stressed, this will be a cinch. If you're not, just think about literally anything happening in the world right now and feel that tension rise!

3 Release the tension with one huge exhale. Notice how fucking good you feel?

4 Now turn your attention to your head and try to release any tension you feel there. Soften your eyes. Unclench your jaw. Turn the volume down on your thoughts.

5 At this point, you should be sinking into the floor with relaxation. Normally, it isn't a great idea to just let an overwhelming force overtake you, but in Savasana, that's the whole point. Let your body feel heavy on the floor. If there are any parts of you that won't behave, focus in on those especially.

6 Do this for as long as you need, but anywhere from five to twenty minutes should do it. When you're chill as a frozen margarita, exit Savasana with a deep breath out and then in. Bring normal but calm movement back—wiggle your toes, move your fingers, do jazz hands—and bend your knees. Roll onto your side and come to a seated position. Congratulations, you're now calm as fuck.

create a sacred space: no haters allowed

Mindfulness isn't supposed to feel like your regular life, so why try to practice it just anywhere? Designate your meditation time as separate from the rest of your day by setting aside a place that's just for you to get your mindfulness on.

1. You don't need an entire room, just a place where no one will bother you. Ideally it's secure, not just for your privacy, but also because meditation is super vulnerable! You're breathing, stretching, and

chanting mantras—that shit is private! Make sure you're somewhere where you can hang a sign on the door that says GONE MANIFESTIN'. A corner? Your hallway? That weird conference room at work no one uses? It's all up to you.

2 If you don't have a ton of space, you can transform it with the stuff you choose to display. If most of the time the corner of your bedroom is for a pile of clothes you'll deal with eventually, maybe you can change the energy a little by adding a candle, crystal, and meditation cushion there.

3 Now that your space is set, don't just barge in whenever. The last thing you want to do is bring your daily stress into your comfortable space. Check in with yourself and your chakras when you enter. Not only will you check your bad vibes at the door, but you'll also figure out what it is you need that day.

EXERCISE 12

schnoz knows best

When was the last time you were grateful your nose wasn't running? Whenever your face gets all stuffy, all you want is clear nasal passages, but once you have them, you totally take them for granted. No more! *Nadi Shodhana* is a breathing pattern designed to REALLY get that schnoz working by getting each nostril to produce long, calming breaths. Here's how:

1. Sit comfortably with your spine straight. Yes, good posture is a drag, but this is the best way to get that breath flowing like fondue in a chocolate fountain.

2. Hold your right hand in *Vishnu mudra* (a hand position where the thumb, ring finger, and pinky are extended, and the other fingers are bent). If you

feel like a fancy lady holding a teacup, that means you're killing it.

3 Close off your right nostril with your right thumb and take a soft breath in through your left nostril.

4 At the top of that breath, close off the left nostril with the right ring finger and exhale through the right nostril. Then breathe back on into the right nostril. Keep repeating and alternating.

5 Do this for two minutes or however long it takes for your breath to feel even more calm and serene than usual, you goddamn mindfulness superstar.

friendly fucking reminder: the nadis

What the fuck are Nadis? They're the reason breathing into your nostrils can feel so damn good. There's been a lot of talk about ki flowing through the body, but the Nadis are the actual tunnels it flows through. The main one goes from the base of your spine to the crown of your head, but two other important ones begin at your spine and end in your nostrils. By doing this kind of breathing you're basically saying, "Hey, life is a highway, and my ki is going to ride it all night long."

earth's got your back

When you get tired, just remember that Earth literally supports billions of people, plants, animals, and weird little fungi all while rotating on an axis that gives us seasons, tides, and all the other great shit we take for granted. If your multitasking abilities extend to being on your phone while eating dinner (no judgment), taking a few cues from Earth's energies is probably a good idea.

1. Sit or lie down and chill—breathe calmly and try to clear your mind.

2. The way you guide yourself through this meditation is with intense visualization, which is just a really fancy way of saying, "Use your fucking imagination!"

3 Start with a simple image of you, barefoot on a stone bench on a grassy hillside. You feel like a kid again, walking barefoot outside before you learned about boring things like tetanus. You sink your feet into the earth beneath you. Germaphobes, this is going to be hard, but believe in yourself.

4 As your feet settle into the earth, imagine them taking root in the soil. Remember those tree guys from Lord of the Rings? You're like that, but way hotter.

5 As you continue to settle into the ground, close your eyes and lift your head. Notice how much straighter you sit with the earth supporting you. Thanks, Earth!

6 Okay, so you've gotten your power from the ground. Now, it's time to open yourself up to the sky. Get your crown chakra ready with a quick sweeping of your aura with your fingers, which is mindfulness speak for brushing your fingers lightly over the top of your head. Imagine there's a canopy of leaves blocking your crown from getting the sunlight it needs and you're bushwhacking all the foliage out of your way. Peacefully. When the clutter is out of the way, let the sun shine on your head and beam through you, all the way to the roots.

EXERCISE 14

balance, bitch!

If you haven't really stretched since elementary school gym class, give *Parsvottanasana* (intense side stretch) a try. Physical balance leads to mental balance and you're really going to need both. Here's how to do it:

1. Standing with your feet apart, place your hands on your hips. Turn your left foot forty-five to sixty degrees and turn your right leg out like you're showing it off. Imagine the universe applauding your gorgeous leg. You deserve it!

2. Take a huge breath in while grounding your feet and using the inhalation to extend your body up all the way! Maybe you thought you were standing up straight but this proves there's always room to go further up. Reflect on how deep that shit is as you continue to stretch.

3. Exhale and turn to face your right leg. Admire your leg once again! Place your hands palm to palm in

reverse prayer position behind your middle back. Revolve your left leg in its socket, turning the front thigh to face forward (don't force or strain it, seriously, it isn't worth it).

4 Inhale and extend your spine so you are looking up—this move is all about positivity and balance, so keep your body strong and your focus up! Exhale and, bending from the hips, swing your body over the right leg. Gaze at your toes. Look, this whole exercise is about admiring your lower body, so really get into it.

5 See if you can balance the forward action of the torso extending over the front leg by pulling your hips back and drawing the top of the thighs and hamstrings up behind you. If you can, you're basically Simone Biles. If you aren't, well, just keep breathing and stretching because it still works!

6 Stay in this pose for a few breaths and then come back up by pressing strongly into your feet. You might feel twisted up, stretched out, and a little less flexible than you remember, but if you feel even a little more balanced, pop the metaphorical champagne! Now, repeat on the other side!

hey anxiety? fuck off

Anxiety does a ton of shitty things to people, but one of the most frustrating is the fact that it can get your breathing out of whack. Breathing is so important in mindfulness, so show anxiety and intense emotions who the fucking boss is with some three-part breaths.

1 Sit comfortably with a long spine. That means sit up straight—if you need to use a chair for your posture, go for it. There's never any shame in needing an assist, whether it's propping yourself up with a pillow or googling how to spell "entrepreneur."

2 Seal your lips and relax your forehead, jaw, and belly.

3. Begin to take steady, long breaths in and out through your nostrils.

4. Let your breath slow down so much that you can feel your belly, rib cage, then chest expand and contract with each inhalation and exhalation. At this point you don't want to be gulping for air like a fish out of water! Just keep breathing deeply at an even rhythm.

5. Here's where things get real. Slo-o-o-o-w down your exhalations. Not just a little; you want them to be even longer than when you inhale. People with strong abs tend to find this a little easier, but consider that people with strong abs also tend to not eat carbs. What the fuck kind of life is that?

6. Keep slowing down. You should practically be exhaling in slow motion. The slower the exhale, the more time you have to release all the shitty feelings holding you down. Anger? Gone. Frustration? Never met her. Anxiety? Who the fuck is that?

7. Continue for three to five minutes. Keep going until you feel like your breath is completely yours again.

EXERCISE 16

vitamin sea

If you're having trouble finding a happy place while meditating, try the beach, bitch! If you've never been to a beach or don't have fond memories, don't sweat it. Regular beachgoers will tell you that it isn't always easy to relax near the water. There are seagulls trying to steal your sandwiches, jellyfish with their tentacles aimed right at you, and leathery old men wandering around in Speedos. Ditch the reality and focus on the pleasant parts for a mindful getaway that will tide you over until you can do the real thing.

1 Lie down in whatever position is comfortable and shut your eyes. Start breathing the way you usually do when you meditate—rhythmic, steady breaths.

2 This is where the fun begins. Imagine yourself lying on your belly on a glass-bottomed boat that is gently gliding through the water. Let yourself look down through the bottom of the boat. You can see

either the really gnarly shit under the sea like the *Titanic* or those freaky fish that don't need eyes, or just coral reefs and schools of colorful fish going about their fish lives.

3 As your visualization gets more vivid, you should feel increasingly connected to the ocean. The motion of the waves, the feel of the water, the cute fish—not even jellyfish can kill your vibe.

4 Let the boat melt away and envision yourself in the water. You take to it like Michael fucking Phelps. Maybe you even make a dolphin noise. Who knows?

5 When you've had enough, let yourself swim back to shore and slowly open your eyes. Re-engage with the sights, sounds, and smells of the world around you. See if you feel more refreshed after your mini-vacation.

be a sunny bitch

The sun is a source of power and the reason our planet can support life. Many ancient religions were based on sun worship. On a sunny day, you can find calm and peace through the warmth of the sun. The sun is a natural healer and will vitalize your body, fend off depression, and keep your energy balanced. If you live in a region where sunshine is sparse, you can substitute light therapy by sitting under special lamps designed for this purpose.

❶ Before you start thinking about the shit you have to do today, get some natural light if you can. It's good for you, like a gym membership that you'll actually use.

2️⃣ While you let the light soak in, close your eyes and focus on your breathing, and being in the moment. Remember that just by being alive, you're probably fucking awesome at breathing. As your breathing grows steady and rhythmic, imagine the sun wrapping you up in a warm hug. Hug the sun right back.

3️⃣ If you're doing it right, you'll feel like your own badass little sunbeam. Think about the day ahead and how you can bring warmth and light to your plans, even if they involve something unpleasant, like asking your landlord to fix the sink, or putting on yoga pants.

4️⃣ Say thank you to the sun for sharing her light, and please, for the love of all that is good, put on some sunscreen.

EXERCISE 18
let your left nostril shine

Like most people, you probably don't know shit about your left nostril. It turns out, the little guy is a cosmic miracle! It connects with the moon to be a source of comforting energy when you need it and helps expel excess pitta for total balance. Today, we salute the left nostril.

1. Sit comfortably with your back straight.

2. Hold up your right hand and fold your index and middle fingers into the palm of your hand, keeping the thumb, ring finger, and pinky extended.

3. Use your thumb to seal your right nostril. Take a huge, complete breath through ol' lefty.

4. Seal your left nostril with your ring finger, release your thumb, and exhale out of the right nostril.

5. Repeat this sequence—inhaling through your left nostril and exhaling through your right. Do three of these and finish the cycle with a regular breath that uses both nostrils. Repeat if you need to—since the left nostril takes in all kinds of good energy, you're using this exercise to channel it all over the damn place, so don't skimp.

EXERCISE 19

perform a body scan

You know where you physically are, but do you know where you *really are*? Like, really, man? Body scans can feel tedious, but taking account of how each part of your body is feeling helps you reconnect with yourself during days when your brain is somewhere else.

1 Lie down on your back, with your legs outstretched comfortably on the floor.

2 Take a slow, deep inhale through your nose and exhale through your mouth. Make it a really good exhale—a *money* exhale. Release all your tension.

3 Commence the scan! Start with a focus on your feet. Left toes. Right toes. The arches. The heels. Keep moving this slowly up through your whole body: legs, torso, arms, the whole shebang.

4 As you zero in on different parts of your body, *really* notice them, dammit. When you notice tension, take a deep breath and focus on letting that shit go. You know by now that you shouldn't let stress live rent-free in your head but don't let it freeload in your body as well.

EXERCISE 20

massage
your heart
(not as gross as it sounds)

It turns out massaging your heart isn't just part of CPR! A standing spinal twist straight from yoga brings all the benefits of a defibrillator straight to you.

1 Stand with your feet parallel, shoulder-width apart. Don't overthink it and get crazy trying to measure the exact width of your shoulders. Just chill, relaxing your arms by your sides.

2 This next part sounds like the instructions to the Cha Cha Slide, but if you're patient with yourself it will all come together. Exhale as you slowly draw your navel back toward your spine and rotate from

your waist, turning your rib cage and shoulders to the left. Next, keep that pelvis stationary and feet flat with the floor as you bend your elbows and bring your right hand to your left shoulder and your left arm behind your back. Look over your left shoulder.

3 Massage time! Rev your engine by exhaling and gently twisting to the right. Let your arms be soft and relaxed as you twist so one hand taps the front of your shoulder and the back of the other taps your lower back.

4 Create a steady rhythm as you rotate from side to side, keeping your arms relaxed at your sides coordinating your breath with your movements. Keep your spine relaxed and tall as you move. Stay focused on strong exhalations and pick up the pace to a comfortable, steady pace. Don't think about how this is massaging your heart because you'll gross yourself out. Just keep making calm and strong movements.

5 After ten to thirty repetitions, gradually slow the movement down until you return to stillness.

sometimes you just have to get out of bed

People always talk about how yoga is good for depression and it is such a pain in the ass. When you're depressed the last thing you want to do is sit through a sweaty class where some kombucha chugger keeps telling you to breathe. There's no denying that yoga does help, but the key is to take it one pose at a time. This is an easy pose to boost your mood, and remember, if you want to crawl right back in bed after doing it, that's okay.

1. Sit cross-legged on the floor, cup your fingertips by your hips, and lightly lift your buttocks, stretching your torso up. Then lower your butt. This is what is known as "yogic twerking."

2. Bend your elbows and place the back of your hands on top of your thighs, close to your hips, and lift your spine up while keeping your butt firmly on the floor. No twerking this time, just stillness.

3. Sit in this position for a hot second, just inhaling and keeping your spine long. Exhale slowly and carefully while bending your neck. For bonus points you can bend at the seventh cervical vertebra where your neck meets your shoulders, but if you want to just slowly bring your chin to your chest and shut your eyes, no one is going to care.

4. Stay in this position for five minutes. Okay, fine, maybe five is too long. Try three. Ugh, okay, two. After two minutes, you can lie down and relax.

EXERCISE 22
highway to the zen zone

Sometimes you have everything ready to go—yoga mat, crystals, glass of tea that looks like mud—but you just can't stop your mind from wandering. Don't freak out. Just like everything else, it all comes down to breathing. Try this:

1. Create a comfortable space to let your brain get all the craziness out. Lie down with a blanket or pillow under your head and close your eyes. Breathe and let your mind roam like an old-timey cowboy.

2. When you're ready, breathe in deeply and follow with a long, easy exhale. No straining or pretending you took in more air than you did! Meditation doesn't respond well to cheating.

3. Inhale and return to normal breathing for three complete breaths.

4. Exhale the breath completely. Resume the cycle of deep inhalation and long exhalation, followed by three normal breaths. Repeat this pattern three times. Open your eyes and look around you. The Zen is nigh.

almost as good as caffeine

This is for when you get really draggy. Like, 3 p.m. on a Wednesday, can't look at any emails, thinking about napping in your boss's office draggy. This is drawn from Pranayama, an ancient technique that's basically a nuclear option when it comes to directing energy into the body.

1. Sit or lie down in a comfortable position with your spine supported.

2. Close your eyes or fix your gaze softly on a still object.

3. Inhale so deeply you can see your belly expand. Start slow—there's more breathing to come.

4. Keep inhaling. Instead of focusing on just your belly, focus on your whole torso.

5. It's the final stretch of the inhale so don't wimp out! Keep breathing in and feel this huge breath expand to your back. Feel it all the way behind your shoulder blades.

6. Okay, *now* you can exhale slowly, feeling each part of you—rib cage, torso, shoulders—relax. Now, go tackle that inbox.

take a picture. it will last longer

What if there was a way to use *Instagram* for good instead of evil? You can use images as tools that further pave the path to mental stability or you can keep looking at the wedding photos of people you hate. The choice is yours!

1 Find a picture of something you really love. It doesn't have to be somewhere you've been or even somewhere real—if Narnia calms you down, well, hello Mr. Tumnus.

2 Place this image where you can see all the details. It's best if you have it printed out, but if you have to use your phone, airplane mode is your friend. Don't let the group chat distract you while you're finding your bliss, you know?

③ Focus your attention on the image. Try to take in more than just the physical stuff in the photo—look deeper and notice things like light and shadow, or the subtle differences between colors. Draw on that one semester of art history you took. You'll feel like wearing a beret when you're done, you artsy bitch.

④ Slowly close your eyes and in your mind's eye, try to see the same image in as much detail as you can. Open your eyes and see if what was in the picture matches your mental image. If it isn't a perfect match, who fucking cares? Try again. The worst that can happen is that you meditate on the image for a little longer. Keep going and your mind's eye will be seeing in twenty-twenty in no time.

evaluate your relationships

Bad relationships aren't just unpleasant while we're in them. They have this super fun way of affecting our interactions with every other member of the human race until we die. Cool, right? No, not cool. While therapy is obviously the best solution, this list of questions is a quick way to evaluate where you are right now. It can get heavy, so have tissues on hand and make sure you're in a place where you're comfortable tackling this stuff.

1. As you answer these questions, think about how your answers shape you and what you want. What is a nonnegotiable deal breaker? What actually isn't that big a deal in retrospect? You might end up surprising yourself.

- How did people speak to each other in your family? Like a fifties sitcom, with lots of family dinners and people calling each other "slugger," or was it like a nineties sitcom with everyone screaming at each other?

- Were people open emotionally in your family or were they the kind who loved to bottle things up only to have them explode at family gatherings? While this habit makes for memorable weddings, no one can really call it healthy.

- How was conflict handled in your family? Did people slam doors? Yell? Write pointed letters to local newspapers under a fake name?

- Did anyone use love or intimacy as a means to manipulate? Do your parents know how to guilt you into just about anything and do you know how to say no?

2. Once you've thought through the answers to these questions, say aloud or to yourself, "I am okay and it is okay." Even if you don't feel okay right now at this exact moment, you will be. Knowing yourself is half the battle.

stay in the moment
(and get shit done)

Once you're all in (or even mostly all in) with the Law of Attraction, it can be hard to stay in the present. Why bother with daily life right now when you have the idea of the future ahead of you? Future you is going to kick ass. Everything will be perfect!

This is a fun fantasy, but it totally blocks you from the moment, which is a major mindfulness no-no. Even when the present totally blows, it's always healthier to engage with it. Channel some of the mental energy you're spending on things that haven't happened yet and use breath work to bring it into your body. It's an espresso shot for your chakras that gives you the energy needed to actually get shit done to reach your goals.

1. Sit quietly, concentrating on your breathing. Try to clear away any distracting thoughts about anything that isn't happening right now or directly impacting you.

2. Take an especially long and deep breath, and notice the way the air fills your belly, ribs, and chest. Exhale it all out slowly. The exhale should last longer than the inhale, so be patient with your breath. Get ready to do it again.

3. On the next inhale, use the power of visualization to imagine the air flowing in reaching differing chakras. Imagine your body like a switchboard that lights up the deeper you breathe. It floats down from your busy brain to light up your throat, which allows you to say the things you need to say. From there, it travels to your heart, connecting you with the people around you even when it's with your weird neighbor who never smiles. Take the breath to the solar plexus for strength. This helps you continue living your best life even when it's hard, which you know it can be. Finally, light up the sacral chakra for a burst of creativity so you can handle everything life throws at you with flair.

fix your damn back

Literally everything causes back pain. You can't win, but dammit, you can TRY. By shifting your focus to your chakras, you can at least make sure your body is ready to heal once you finally figure out what's fucking up your back.

1 Sit or lie down, even if it takes your rickety body forever to get into that position. Place a rolled-up towel comfortably in the natural curve of your spine.

2 Begin with a deep, long inhale and slow exhale, repeated several times. Think of the breath traveling from your sacral chakra up through your throat.

3 Let your inhalations get a little deeper. Instead of starting in the sacral chakra, the breath is now beginning at the root chakra. As you take in air, imagine it hitting every chakra on its way up and clearing away any dust it finds.

4 You're maybe wondering, "What about my crown chakra?!" It's not invited to this party! Your crown is your link to the world around you and your focus needs to be on your body.

EXERCISE 28
look away from the fucking screen

You may not think you can be away from your phone or computer for long, but dammit, you should. That shit is not good for your eyes! While taking a much-needed break from your screen, use some therapeutic movements to show your peepers that you care. Here is an exercise to give your eyes some much-needed rest.

1 Start by gleefully rubbing your hands together like a cartoon villain to create some HEAT.

2 When your hands are sufficiently warmed, shut your eyes and place your palms over the eyes. Not to blow your mind here, but this technique is called "palming the eyes." Because it's your palms ON YOUR EYES.

3 Now open your eyes and look down. If you've ever been accused of having resting bitch face, this is your time to shine. Side-eye to the left. Side-eye to the right. Roll your eyes. When it comes to stretching your eyes, bitchy is better.

(try to) **be a morning person**

Do you wake up to the sound of birds chirping and prepare yourself a wholesome meal of free-range eggs? Do you wait for little woodland creatures to help dress you? Do you lie in bed and stare at your phone while losing track of time and then eventually spray dry shampoo all over yourself in some approximation of a shower? If what you're doing seems to be working for you, that's great, but if you're looking for a new way to open up the day, the basics of Ayurveda are here to help.

1. Use a tongue scraper to clear all the nasties from the night before off your tongue. Sure, also use a toothbrush, but with a tongue scraper your mouth is going to feel truly clean.

2. Use a neti pot to clear your nasal passages.

3 Use nasal oil to keep the nasal passages moist, creating less inviting conditions for bacteria or allergens. There are special oils made for this purpose, so don't get wild with the Crisco.

4 Put an Ayurvedic ear oil in your ears to keep them healthy. Again, look into the kind of oils that are best for this, or else you're looking at an awkward visit to an ENT.

5 Spray rose water in your eyes to stop them from burning or itching. If this freaks you out, you can just give your face a quick misting with rose water. You'll smell like a garden and feel classy as fuck.

6 Massage your entire body with oil. Aside from being a truly luxurious way to moisturize, Ayurvedic oils are designed to get your blood flowing. Remember, your skin is an organ too and needs some goddamn respect.

7 Drink a glass of warm water. If you want, you can run it through a filter filled with ground-up coffee beans for a fun twist (it's coffee, the twist is coffee).

8 Do some of the breathing exercises found in this book!

hearing without headphones

LIFE IS TOO FUCKING LOUD! Sorry, *life is too fucking loud.* Not only are we faced with things like elevator music and people who don't keep their phone on silent (seriously, who does that?), but we're also a huge part of the problem! When we hear something we don't like, we can just drown it out with things we do like—music, audiobooks, those videos where a pair of disembodied hands makes food superfast. This is fine, but it's also worth it to give existing alongside these sounds a try.

1. In your most comfortable meditation posture, close your eyes. Begin to listen.

2. Start with the farthest sounds you can identify. For example, if you hear water running from a faucet down the hallway, try to isolate that. For those of you in loud-ass neighborhoods, try to focus on the farthest away calming sound you can pick up on. Downstairs neighbors and motorcycles? No. Water and birds chirping? Hell yes!

3. Now go to the next sound that presents itself to you. Is your radiator rattling? Is your cat fucking shit up in the other room? Focus in on it. Maybe go check on that cat to make sure it isn't eating paper again.

4. Continue listening to sounds that are even closer to you: fans, clocks—there's bound to be tons of shit surrounding you that you never even noticed made a sound. Keep listening, and then slowly tune everything out. Eventually, you want the only thing you hear to be your own heartbeat. Enjoy it and resist the urge to freestyle to it.

write a badass haiku

Meditation can feel like torture sometimes, what with the no talking thing, but a little creativity makes it feel *less* like a chore and *more* like something nice you're doing for yourself. You know how most vegetables are better with ranch? Writing a haiku is the ranch dressing on the celery of meditation. And look, creative expression doesn't have to be a huge commitment. Sometimes it's as simple as three lines and seventeen syllables. That's right: It's motherfucking haiku time.

1. **Pick a subject.** It can be a feeling, a memory, something that makes you feel calm, something you're pissed about, or just something that makes you happy, like a dog wearing sunglasses and a party hat. Whatever it is you want to say, let that shit fly. There are no bad subjects to write about.

2. **Keep it short!** We're talking three lines with five syllables in the first line, seven in the second, and five more in the third. Don't make yourself crazy, though—the world won't end if you use an extra syllable or four. Who's going to know?

3. **Share your haikus, if you want.** If you want to keep your ode to putting on pajamas after work under wraps, that's your business. However, if you want to share "Kaitlin, I get that / Whole thirty sounds promising / But please, make it stop" with a certain unnamed friend, go for it.

friendly fucking reminder: look around

Most haikus tend to be about nature, so if you're short on inspiration, draw on the world around you. What color are the leaves on the trees? Is it hot or cold outside? You're smart; you get it.

set your intention

You may have tried overnight oats, dream journals, and early-morning yoga, but there's one more thing you should try to start your day: swapping out your typical a.m. aimlessness for some intention setting. Here's how:

1. Write your intention on a piece of paper or in your phone—somewhere you can see it throughout the day.

2. Inhale and say your intention, like, "I am supported by the world around me, no matter how many meetings I go to today that could have just as easily been emails." The support of the earth underneath you is an affirmation that yes, that really could have been solved if your boss just read the whole thread.

3. Repeat the intention three times with your eyes closed, envisioning it to be true. The repetition really does matter! When you tell yourself "I am human garbage" over and over, you start to FEEL like human garbage. Change the channel in your brain to something nice.

4. Repeat your intention several times throughout the day.

EXERCISE 33
salute your root

The one chakra that you should absolutely, 100 percent, not ignore is your root chakra. Think of the root chakra like your most responsible friend—if it gets blackout drunk, god only knows what happens to everyone else at the party. Keep your root chakra happy with a little *prana mudra*, which is supposed to bring it extra life force. Here's how:

1. Hold both hands so that the palms face up, and curl the ring finger and pinky finger of each hand in and touch your thumb on that same hand, like you're giving the world's laziest peace sign.

2. Keep the pointer and middle fingers straight.

3. Hold this for fifteen minutes, three times a day. It'll pass sooooo slowly at first but it's worth it. Remember, the root chakra is the *money* chakra. It needs your love.

get it done in five minutes

If you think you don't have time to check in with yourself during the day, think again. You can cram all the mindful goodness you need into just five minutes. It could end up being the best fucking five minutes you spend all day.

1 Log off the computer—don't just shut your laptop or dim the brightness; that's the easy way out. Close EVERY tab on your computer. Log out of your email. Stop stalking that girl you hated in middle school on *Facebook*. None of this shit serves you!

2 Turn off your cell phone. No, not airplane mode. Turn that shit off and place it across the room. It's harsh, but if you're only going to do this for five minutes, you need to commit.

3 Sit down. You should feel unburdened without your computer and phone, not more anxious! If you're anxious about things or messages you're missing, remind yourself that it's only five minutes. It's pretty much the length of "My Heart Will Go On." You can do this.

4 Start by focusing on your breathing. This exercise isn't about any fancy breathing patterns, just taking inventory. Don't judge the way you're breathing; just keep doing it.

5 What are you thinking about while you're breathing? Work? Evening plans? Celine Dion? (Sorry.) As each thought arises, imagine exhaling it away with each breath out. This is the gentlest way to say "bye, bitch" to a busy mind.

6 Once it's been five minutes, take one last ceremonial breath. Don't just get up and run back to your phone. This is your moment, dammit!

pick up
your shit!

Clutter has a way of sneaking up on you. You start off with an empty space and next thing you know you somehow have every receipt ever provided by man or machine taking up space in your home. The problem with clutter is that it doesn't just crowd up your space, but it fucks with your mind too, literally blocking the natural flow of ki. Since ki is the life force of literally everything, you can guess how bad this is. While you don't need to turn your house inside out and scrub down every surface, a little bit of mindful tidying never hurts.

1. **Pick one cluttered space.** Maybe you have too many bottles and tubes of crap in the bathroom or a pile on the floor of your closet that looks like

it might come alive. Remember, no need to tackle everything at once.

2 **Start tossing shit!** Say goodbye to each item as you let it go. Make sure you finish the job and don't just leave the stuff you're getting rid of on the floor or in another pile. Remove it from the area 100 percent! You are a trash-free zone!

3 **Once you're done, take in the new space.** Pat yourself on the back for being so fucking organized and gear up to tackle the next space! Suck it, Marie Kondo, mindful cleaning has a new boss.

friendly fucking reminder: out with the old, in with the new (then out with the new, in with more stuff)

People tend to beat themselves up over clutter, especially when they find themselves in a cycle of throwing shit out just to accumulate more. This cycle can be found everywhere in nature—the tides go in and go out, snakes shed their skin, and you can't stop buying different kinds of shampoo. It's okay to make this cycle a part of your life!

invest in your breath

Your body is going to breathe whether you think about it or not, so why not try to make it the best breath possible? Think of it like sleeping—you need to sleep, but you don't just lie on the floor with an old towel covering you when you get tired. You put on comfortable clothes, brush your teeth, hunker down under the covers, and *then* drift off. Dirgha breath, a yogic breathing pattern, is a routine to raise your awareness of your breathing and improve the quality of your breath throughout the day.

dirgha breath

1 Kneel down or sit. If you choose to kneel, make sure you're comfortable. Invest in a meditation cushion or go full X Games and put on some kneepads.

2 Place your hands on your stomach. Inhale deeply and feel your hands rise as you inhale. Exhale and feel them fall. Keep things this simple for the first few breaths.

3 Switch up your hand placement by putting them on the sides of your ribs. Instead of focusing on making your stomach rise and fall, breathe so that you feel your ribs expand outward. Notice how different your breath feels when you move your ribs instead of your stomach.

4 Change the hand placement again, this time with one hand on the upper chest and collarbones (décolletage, if you're fancy) and the other on the back of your shoulders, right below your neck. Breathe in and focus on feeling both those places expand. This isn't easy, so be patient with yourself.

5 Now try to do each of these breaths in a row, focusing on your stomach, ribs, and upper chest. Notice how much deeper and more effective each breath feels compared to your old regular breaths.

take a cooling breath

No matter how different we are—left-handed or right-handed, morning people or night owls, vegans or people who can shut up—we can all agree that it feels fucking awful when it's too hot to breathe well. Luckily, because you're a wellness expert in touch with your body, you have a secret weapon: using your own breath to keep yourself cool.

1. Sit comfortably with a long spine. Remember, your spine doesn't stop at your neck. Keep your head straight and balanced. No half-assing!

2. Purse your lips and stick your tongue out. Take a selfie if you want because let's face it—that is a primo selfie pose that should not go to waste.

3. If you can curl your tongue, flex your genetic gift and furl that sucker up. If not, remember that you're perfect just as you are, and keep that shit relaxed.

4. Inhale slowly and feel the air go over your tongue— just having your tongue out in contact with the air should already keep you cool. You'll feel a kinship with all dogs who have ever stuck their head out a window.

5. Relax your tongue and draw it back into your mouth. Seal your lips, holding in all that cool air. Now exhale super slowly.

6. You know what's coming next: Repeat! Do this four or five times until you feel sufficiently chilled out.

EXERCISE 38
warrior pose badass

Civilization is a good thing, but sometimes you just want to feel like a goddamn ancient warrior ready to kick some ass. This is where the *Virabhadrasana* pose, known as the warrior pose, comes in. A few seconds of this brings you from meek victim of modernity to badass ancient god of war. (For you yoga nerds, this is technically warrior pose 2.)

1 Stand up straight and proud, and extend both your arms from the side of your body. Really stretch them—don't be afraid to take up some fucking space!

2 Rotate your left foot in and your right foot out. Take a deep breath and bring your right knee over your right ankle by bending your hip, knee, and ankle. Don't put too much pressure on your knee—power comes when you feel comfortable and sturdy.

3 Gaze toward your right hand and admire it. That is the hand of a WARRIOR. Hold the pose. Come out of it by straightening your right leg and turning your foot back inward. Repeat on the left side.

EXERCISE 39
balance your afternoon

An afternoon cup of coffee and a protein-packed lunch can't undo the simple fact that the hours between 2 p.m. and 6 p.m. feel like they take roughly thirty years off your life. Ayurveda knows why you want to collapse in the afternoon; it turns out that's the time when your vata dosha is most dominant, so if you don't respond well to vata, it's going to be a rough afternoon. Here's how to handle it.

1. Remember all the contrasts in Ayurveda? Try to put them into practice here. Vata is cold, so you'll want to drink something warm. Hot tea with lemon! A cappuccino! Hot cocoa! It's literally that simple.

2. If it's warm outside, go out and take a quick stroll. Not only do you get to pump yourself up with some sunlight, but changing the scenery is also a great chance to ground yourself.

3. Eat something that will make you feel better, not worse. Vata in particular finds balance with whole grains and protein, so try to find something in that category. Pop-Tarts may seem like a good idea, but your vata will disagree.

sit for refreshment

If you've ever been on a phone or laptop, you know how easy it is to lose track of time. You log in to respond to one text about dinner plans, and next thing you know a combination of *Netflix* bingeing, social media stalking, and plain old fucking around means that hours can pass before you even know it. This isn't a bad thing, and you don't need to become one of those people who're like "I don't even own a TV" in order to fix it. By adopting a few new practices to make your butt-in-chair time a bit more intentional, you can rejuvenate your mind and body in between work spreadsheets or episodes of *The Great British Baking Show* (or both!).

1. Try to always sit at a desk when you're on the computer. Lying in bed with a laptop on your belly is one of the forms of heaven on earth, but let's not be too proud to admit it isn't exactly a pose for productivity. Sitting with your feet on the floor and your back supported promotes a sense of groundedness and focus.

2. Make sure you aren't slouching. You don't need to balance a pile of books on your head like a Victorian schoolgirl or develop abs of steel. Just placing a cushion at the curve of your back makes it easier to sit up straight for longer; no sit-ups required.

3. Keep your arms supported. Carpal tunnel is E for Everyone, so keep your wrists comfy with a little bit of cushioning.

4. Try to keep your computer at eye level if you can. Use a phone book (if those still exist) or a shoebox to add some extra height under your laptop if you need it. Otherwise, you'll be craning your neck like a giraffe instead of focusing on the stuff that matters.

change your mood

Having a looming deadline or standing item on your to-do list can feel a little like slowly drowning in quicksand or watching a huge wave build up before it crashes over you. This quick grounding exercise is designed to help you break intimidating things down into manageable chunks that make even those most daunting tasks feel doable.

1. Stop what you're doing (or not doing), and write down whatever you want to be doing instead. It doesn't have to be noble or even particularly good for you; it can just be "watching a movie where everyone is wearing a hoop skirt" or "smelling all the fancy lotions at Sephora."

2 Provided that the task you're putting off isn't urgent (if you're paying a bill, ignore this and write that check), take inventory of the steps and resources needed to make this happen. Do you need access to a car? Your roommate's HBO password? Make sure to account for every step.

3 As you look at the steps, you'll probably notice how achievable it all seems. Most of the time, it's downright easy. Now break down the thing you're currently doing into the same series of steps. You'll probably notice the same thing.

friendly fucking reminder: words matter

Just because anything with the words "live, laugh, love" embroidered on it makes you break out in hives doesn't mean all motivational quotes will. If you manage to find one you like, whether it's from a movie, a fortune cookie, or—god forbid—*Pinterest*, write it down. Make sure you keep it somewhere you can see it and tack it up where you need it most.

EXERCISE 42
meditate with malas

What the fuck are malas and why are they so magical? They're a string of 108 beads that you use to focus while meditating. The more you use a mala, the more of your vibrations, energy, and intentions it holds.

1. Get in a comfortable position for meditation, in a quiet spot. Have your malas with you.

2. Choose a mantra. If you're coming up empty, try some of these: "I am enough." "I am grateful." "I am a badass." Whatever brings you peace! Namaste!

3. Start with the bead next to the "guru" bead, which is the bead at the knot. Hold the first bead in between your thumb and middle finger. Slowly start moving each bead on the string between those fingers. With each bead you move, say your mantra again.

4. In order to keep the energy flowing right, don't cross the guru bead if you want to go another round with the mala. Make like Missy Elliott and put your thing down, flip it, and reverse it, reciting your mantra in the opposite direction. This keeps the energy in the beads consistent and lets you do as much as you need.

shake it off

From the ancient words of "The Hokey Pokey" to the modern prophecies of Taylor Swift, sometimes you just need to shake it off. A quick burst of physical activity clears your head and re-centers you when shit weighs you down.

1. Stand up where you are and plant your feet firmly on the ground.

2. Now lift one foot at a time and shake your leg while you inhale and exhale three times. (If balancing is tricky for you, hold on to the back of a chair so you don't fall.)

3. After you shake out both legs, shake out your arms for three long breaths. Do a full body shimmy like a pop goddess and bam! You shook that shit off.

stop dreading the morning with sun salutes

Maybe you don't associate the sun with particularly good times. Getting out of your cozy bed, tending to gnarly sunburns, or just sweating through a dope outfit can make you a certified sun hater. This yoga sequence is used in the morning to get you ready for the day—even total vampires can find something to like about it.

1. Stand with feet hip-width apart and parallel. Distribute the weight evenly between the balls and heels of each foot. Stand as tall as you can—if you're already tall, become an Amazon. If you're short, finally make it to 5'9". Keep breathing calmly, using

your breath to build a rhythm you can work with for the rest of the movement.

2 Inhale and raise the arms out to the sides and up overhead. Press down through the feet, lift out of the waist, and lengthen the fingertips to the sky. Wave to the sun with a quick "hey!"

3 Exhale and swan dive forward, sweeping the arms out to the sides as you hinge forward from the hips. Place both hands on the ground or shins in a forward fold. We're barely into the exercise, so don't get crazy with the stretching just yet if you aren't super bendy.

4 Inhale, press down through the hands and feet, look forward, and lengthen the spine, lifting up halfway into a jackknife position. From here, take another breath and return to your forward fold.

5 Bending the knees, bring the palms to the ground. If you've never touched your toes before, feel free to frame this as a victory even though both knees are bent. The attitude is gratitude; get into it.

6 Inhale and step the left foot back into a lunge. Sweep the arms forward and overhead. You should

feel particularly majestic at this point as you sink deeply into this powerful pose.

7 Okay, there's still more to go, so stay with it. Exhale and sweep down again, taking the palms back to the ground. From there, step the right foot back so you're in push-up position.

8 Do a fancy little yoga push-up in this position. This isn't gym class and there are no jocks to bully you, so if you find push-ups easier while on the knees, go for it.

9 Plant the hips and palms into the ground and arch your back up. Think of how a cat stretches.

10 Exhale, curl the toes under, press palms into the ground, and lift the hips toward the sky. Breathe deeply in this pose. This is the toughest part. Stay upright.

11 Inhale and step the left foot between the hands for a lunge. You may need to reach back and help the foot step all the way forward. Let the arms sweep forward and up again. This pose is all about reaching toward the sky.

12 Exhale, sweep the hands to the ground, and step the right foot beside the left. Place the hands alongside both feet or on the shins.

13 Inhale and look while you lift the chest coming into the jackknife pose again.

14 Release back down. Gently press the belly toward the thighs and the heart toward the shins. If you're having trouble keeping up with the barrage of instructions, continue to take it at a slow pace that's comfortable for you.

15 You're nearly at the finish line. Keep the strength going through the feet and legs, and sweep both arms out to the sides as you inhale again. Press all the way back up to standing, lifting yourself up with the palms touching above your head.

16 Exhale and lower the palms. Take a deep breath and congratulate yourself.

17 There's good news and bad news. The bad news? You have to repeat all this again with the other leg. The good news? You'll feel great afterward.

slay your day with lion's breath

This one goes out to all you kapha types out there who need a little more balance in your system. Even on a busy day, you can still find some time for some quick *Simhasana*, aka Lion's Breath. Use this move to relieve tension in your chest, energize your mind, and channel Nala from *The Lion King*.

1 Sit down or kneel. Don't do this on your bed. You need a hard surface like the floor or the yoga mat you haven't used in seven months so you can really ground yourself. That won't be possible if you cozy up in your nest of throw pillows and *Netflix*.

2 Close your mouth and take deep breaths in and out of your nostrils. Keep breathing. Tell yourself you're really fucking good at breathing.

3 Place your hands on your thighs with your fingers splayed out. Some people say to think of a cat spreading its claws, but it's also useful to imagine yourself as Stevie Wonder about to play some jazzy piano.

4 Inhale deeply through your nose as you draw your belly inward and press your chest forward, arching your upper back. Think about how statues look, and go for that. Lift your chin, open your eyes wide, and gaze upward at the spot between the eyebrows. You won't be able to see it, but trying is half the battle.

5 Open your mouth and stick out your tongue. Stretch the tip of your tongue down toward the chin, contract your swallowing muscles, and slowly exhale while whispering a loud, strong "HAAAA" sound. You might feel crazy doing this, but what's worse—feeling crazy while healing yourself or feeling gross because your kapha is getting rowdy?

6 Repeat steps 4 and 5 four to six times. Really lean into that shit—now is not the time for cute, dainty breaths. Get ugly. Be a lion.

try an evening routine

Maybe the whole "morning routine" thing wasn't for you. That's okay! Shine on, you crazy diamond! That doesn't mean Ayurveda has nothing to offer, just that the timing might have been off. Swap out your usual nighttime routine for an evening that prioritizes internal balance and sound sleep. Who knows? Maybe a put-together night will help your mornings too.

1 Try to eat at the same time every evening and really focus on eating. Turn off *The Bachelor*. Put your phone on airplane mode. You'll be surprised how much a little ceremony can spruce up a can of chicken noodle soup.

2 Around 8:30 p.m., do something calming and soothing. Avoid things like reading *Wikipedia*

pages about unsolved mysteries or thinking about literally every single embarrassing thing you've ever done in your life.

3 Remember when you were a kid and your grandma swore by warm milk to get you to sleep and you pretty much laughed in her face? It turns out that a glass of warm milk (dairy or nondairy) can be a ticket to dreamland. Feel free to give it a boost with turmeric, cardamom, cinnamon, rum, vodka, gin, NyQuil. Just call nana in the morning and apologize.

4 Turn your normal evening ablutions into an opportunity to really treat yourself. Instead of just slapping some lotion on, try using an Ayurvedic body oil for some self-massage. Give some love to your feet and the crown of your head while taking calming deep breaths. Not only will you feel calm, but you'll also be ready for flip-flop season in no time.

5 Try to get to bed by 10 p.m. to get the full eight hours of sleep your body needs to function at its best. No need for FOMO here—nothing good ever happens after 10 p.m. on a weeknight anyway.

kick your intention's ass

You set your intention like a fucking boss, but sometimes even the most pointed and powerful intention needs some extra pizzazz in order to manifest. Try taking a few minutes to meditate on your intention when you feel it getting away from you, and give it the kick in the butt it needs.

1. Find some time in your day where you can sneak away. You need a place where you can really focus, so do yourself a favor and leave your phone behind. It's only a few minutes—you'll live.

2. Try to visualize your intention as a physical object or state. For instance, if you want to feel confident, think about a megaphone amplifying your voice with authority. If you want to feel calm, visualize

a serene oasis. If you want to feel powerful, think about "Cell Block Tango" from *Chicago*. You get it.

3 Keep your focus strong as you breathe, and remind yourself why you're thinking about these things in the first place. Blend the reality of why you want it and how your intention can help. Believe with as much confidence as you can that the universe is ready to deliver. If this feels delusional, double down.

4 The more sincere you can be here, the better. Maybe you don't think the universe is listening, but the beautiful thing about not knowing for sure is that you can choose to blindly think a vast and complex series of forces and systems is taking its time just for you. Crazier things have happened! Believe it, and find a new sense of alignment.

EXERCISE 48
cells, meet oxygen

To all you nitpickers, yes, technically all breath oxygenates your cells. Congrats on the AP Bio grade, nerds! Stop dissecting frogs and give this a try.

1. Lie down with a small pillow under your head and neck. Breathe normally and try to relax.

2. Exhale the breath completely—it should feel easy! For your next inhale, make sure to take the breath in slowly. Visualize the air making its way from your nostrils all the way through your body and feel the way your body expands as it takes air in.

3. By now, you should have enough air in you that you feel like a fully inflated parade float. Don't let it all out at once; be as controlled on the release as you were on the inhale.

4. Continue this pattern for two more complete, big breaths. Inhale gently, and then return to normal breathing for three complete breaths.

5. You know the drill: Repeat three more times, ending on an inhalation.

EXERCISE 49
a very touching moment

It's hard to be as attuned to our sense of touch as we should, simply because we're touching stuff literally all the time. Even during peak relaxation, your butt is touching the chair and your feet are touching the ground. Try as we might, we can't escape touch, so we might as well learn to use it more mindfully.

1 For this meditation, use clay, Play-Doh, or some other easily moldable material.

2 Sit in your most comfortable meditation position with your eyes open and bring your focus to your nondominant hand. If you're normally a righty, start by letting ol' lefty have his day in the sun.

3 Use your hand to slowly press into the material, taking time to notice the way it reacts. Does it give in to your touch? Bubble? Flatten? How do your fingers feel? Your palms? Give yourself two minutes to just feel it.

4 After two minutes, close your eyes. Now, turn your focus to the hand you just used, starting at the wrist. Take notice of how each finger feels.

5 Open your eyes and try it with the other hand.

walk with your brain
(and also your feet)

By now, you should be a pro at walking meditation, so now is the time to step it the fuck up. You're going to not just walk, but walk *mindfully*. Instead of focusing on your mind, you're going to focus on the act of walking itself. You can do this anywhere—a long hallway, around a room, even on the world's slowest treadmill if that's your thing.

1. Observe how your heel reaches the ground before the ball of your foot. If it doesn't, consider the fact you may be a living Barbie doll.

2. Be aware of the contact between the sole of your foot and the ground. You may need to be barefoot to really notice this.

3. Notice the texture and quality of the ground. Be eagle-eyed if you're outside—tons of bad shit lurks out there, and nothing kills the vibe faster than the sudden realization you just stepped in something gross.

4. Feel the shift in weight as you transfer from one leg to the other and marvel at how your body keeps you upright whether you're doing walking meditation or waddling like a penguin as a joke while you're drunk.

5. Observe where your center of gravity is with each step you take. Try to remember which chakra corresponds to it. Use this opportunity to practice self-kindness when you forget.

EXERCISE 51

death, taxes, and trees

They say the only things you can count on are death and taxes, but unfortunately there's no W-9 pose, and corpse pose is so simple you don't really need instructions. Instead, find some stability by emulating the third most reliable thing: a good old tree. Tree pose is a great way to strengthen the body, steady the mind, and build concentration.

1 Stand in *Tadasana* (see Exercise 60), with feet hip-width apart and firmly pressing into the floor.

2 Shift your weight onto the left foot.

3 Bring the sole of the right foot to rest on the inner ankle of the left foot. The knee should point outward. Breathe as evenly as you can. Even if you

aren't naturally the most balanced person in the world, you can maintain this pose.

④ Being careful to hold your balance, slide the right foot up the leg (pausing at the knee or upper inner thigh). Press the foot into the leg for a little more support.

⑤ Don't freak out and go flying all over the place! Instead, gaze on a steady point in front of you and keep your eyes softly fixed on it.

⑥ When you feel stable, raise the arms into a V position overhead and relax the shoulders. Holy shit, you're doing it!

⑦ Hold this posture for a few more breaths, focusing the gaze and the mind.

⑧ Exit this posture the same way you came into it. Exhale and lower the arms, and then slide the foot back down the leg. Redistribute your weight so it's even between both firmly planted feet. Now, repeat on the other side, you goddamn gorgeous tree!

become a mantra master

It's actually easier to understand mantras by being clear about what they aren't. They aren't mottos or sayings to live your life by, and they aren't prayers, though they might sound like both of these things sometimes. Mantras really only exist to help you meditate, and don't even have to mean anything particularly profound as long as you like how it sounds and can repeat it (which means, yes, the opening line of Lady Gaga's "Bad Romance" is absolutely on the table here).

1. If you're serious about mantra meditation, you're going to say those words hundreds of thousands of times throughout your life (don't double-check the math here), so make sure to pick something you like. Buddhism has some ideas for you if you're stuck, like "*Om mani padme hum*," a classic meditation banger that roughly translates to "Hail to the jewel in the Lotus."

2. Take your mantra for a road test by assuming a tried-and-true meditation position and engaging in some steady, calming breathing.

3. Once your breathing becomes routine, begin saying your mantra. You can speak out loud or repeat it internally, whatever feels more comfortable to do. The goal is to feel the syllables of the mantra rhythmically connect with your breathing.

4. Once you're settled into the groove, keep repeating and breathing until you've had enough.

Om mani padme hum...
...om mani padme hum...

open the reiki floodgates

When you get started with Reiki, it really is all guesswork. This is daunting for a lot of people; after all, the only tools you have to start with are good vibes and your own two hands. Visualizations along with traditional Reiki movements can help you figure out what's what when it comes to moving your ki.

1 Think of the flow of energy as being similar to the way water flows from a tap into a sink. Sometimes you turn the knob softly and water barely trickles out. Other times, you twist *way* too hard and the water pressure almost rips your hand off and ricochets off the sink onto the mirror. The sweet spot is

that gentle flow that washes over you with enough force so you know it's there. This is how you want your energy to flow.

2 Complete the metaphor by imagining yourself as a sink basin (a cute one, obviously). When you perform Reiki on yourself, you're hoping to achieve perfect water pressure to get that healing energy right where you want it.

3 Maybe the sink imagery isn't working for you. That's okay! There are thousands of ways for water to move. Flex your middle school Geography Bee muscles and channel an estuary, shit, maybe even an arroyo if you're up for it. Fuck it, be a fjord! Whatever you are, let Reiki flow!

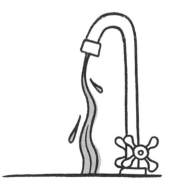

hakini mudra

Hakini mudra is *not* a misspelling of *hakuna matata*. Grow up! This is a very legit way to access your innate knowledge by connecting with your third eye and tapping in to your divine intuition. Here's how to do it:

1 Hold your hands with your palms facing each other, but not touching.

2 Bring the fingertips of the right hand to touch the fingertips of the left, pinky to pinky, ring finger to ring finger, and so on.

3 Direct your gaze upward, which is a nice way of saying, "Roll your eyes bitch!"

4 On the inhale place your tongue against the roof of your mouth.

5 On the exhale, allow the tongue to relax back down.

6 See if you've remembered what you temporarily forgot. This exercise is about opening yourself up to your intuition, which almost always knows something that you don't. If intuition can't help you find your car keys, nothing can.

EXERCISE 55
get up and gassho

Sometimes you don't want to dive right into something semi-sacred like Reiki right after doing something completely mundane, like washing dishes. That's where gassho comes in. Pronounced "gash sho," this is a quick greeting Reiki practitioners do to get themselves into the right mind frame to attract all the healing energies they need.

1 Stand straight and bring your hands together in a prayerlike fashion in front of your heart. Congratulations, you're now doing gassho!

2 If you want to add a little extra to it, take a moment to tap in to the energy around you. Get a feel for the vibe of the room and thank the universe for letting you be a vessel for it. The universe can be a real stickler about manners.

3 Gassho can be as quick or as lengthy as you want. You can use gassho to both begin and end your Reiki sessions, making it a great way to distinguish that time.

steam with essential oils

Knowing anyone who is really, *really* into essential oils can rightfully create some major doubts about these stinky liquids. However, you *can* dabble in the world of EOs without suddenly deciding that they're a good replacement for deodorant. Diffusing an essential oil with some steam does the double duty of bringing some moisture to your face during cold or dry weather while giving your brain some soothing self-care. Don't worry too much about the properties of specific oils as long as you enjoy the scent. You aren't going to give a shit about cedarwood's cleansing properties if you think it smells like a wet dog.

1. Put on a kettle or pot of water and have a towel and your essential oil ready nearby.

2. Once the water boils, pour the steaming water into a large bowl (ten to twelve inches in diameter). Fill the bowl about halfway and add one or two drops of the oil into the bowl. Don't overdo it!

3. Lean your head into the flow of the steam, and put the towel over your head to cover your head and the bowl.

4. Inhale deeply through both nostrils, and then exhale gently through the mouth. Repeat this several times.

5. If you're super congested, go to the old standby of closing one nostril with your finger, and inhaling and exhaling the steam through one nostril at a time.

get into your mind and into your car

Driving is one of those super routine things that can be improved with a dose of mindfulness. Obviously you don't want to go fully meditative while you drive (enjoy your tickets if you do), but much like sitting in your desk chair all day, driving can really fuck with the flow of your ki. If you're frustrated with a bottleneck on the road, consider that the same thing is happening with your chakras. Free up a new spiritual lane.

1. Be deliberate when you get into the car. Sit down slowly, with your back toward the seat. Get a light stretch as you slowly move your hips back to sit down.

2. Once you've sat down, pay attention to how you're situated in the car. How do your fingers feel wrapped around the steering wheel? How does the pressure of the pedals feel under your toes? Does the seat support your back? Driving can be a ki-blocking posture, so make sure you're in touch with your physical self.

3. Feeling good? Great! Once you're seated and your back feels supported, place your hands on the wheel. Make sure you don't have far to reach so you can bend your arms.

4. If you're driving more than fifteen minutes, practice some slight pelvic tilts while driving. For the love of all that is good, please watch the road.

5. To exit the car, simply repeat step 1, but in reverse.

make your break count

If you sit at a desk for eight hours a day, you're an evolutionary miracle. Us humans definitely weren't designed to sit for that long, and even yoga can only do so much to correct our sorry desk-dweller backs. While you may find yourself stretching at your desk throughout the day, add some ceremony and thoughtfulness to the experience. Most things are so boring, so why not treat cracking your back and rolling your shoulders like a goddamn EVENT?

1 Rotate your head side to side, really feeling the rotation in your neck. Rub your hands together to create some heat, and use the heat on your neck or temples.

2 Stand up at least every half hour to move your limbs before sitting back down. This keeps energy flowing and prevents blood clots.

3 Do a quick chakra check-in. Keep some crystals in your desk and use their energy to wake up any lollygaggers that aren't pulling their weight.

4 If a chakra keeps giving you trouble, play a quick game of I spy with your surroundings and find something that's the same color as the chakra in question. When you need a boost, focus on that object and the energy of the color.

friendly fucking reminder: avoid the crystal chaos

Keep it simple when you're buying a crystal for the first time and let your intuition guide you. While there are a ton of guides and friendly gray-haired salespeople who can help you find some polished opalite chunk perfectly attuned to your needs, the amount of information out there can feel seriously overwhelming. It's fine to just pick one that you think is pretty and feels good in your hand.

perform the so hum meditation

Maybe you don't want to reinvent the wheel when it comes to mantras. Maybe you've invented a few wheels and they aren't really getting you anywhere. Maybe you just want to use the most trustworthy wheel of all time, like the kind the pioneers used to cross the plains. If that's the case, all you need are two words: *So Hum*. Commonly translated as "I am that I am," So Hum is a reminder of a fact we sometimes forget: We exist. It might feel super stoner-y to marvel over this fact, but if you've ever watched stoned people make a sandwich, you know that they can have some pretty good ideas.

1. Sit in a comfortable meditation posture, paying special attention to the connection between your body and the ground. You're going to want to feel rooted to the universe for this. So Hum-ing into the void is an existential crisis waiting to happen.

2. Take a deep inhale, and let out a long exhale. Keep breathing, and start making your exhale longer than your inhale.

3. When you feel you've reached a good place with your breathing, close your eyes and bring your hands together in a prayer position at your heart chakra.

4. As you breathe in, imagine the syllable "So," and as you breathe out, imagine the syllable "Hum." Try to get to a point where you aren't even conscious of trying to add the words "so" and "hum" to each breath. You are So. You are Hum. You are so good at So Hum. You'll want to do this for however long it is you usually meditate, whether its five minutes or twenty. If the rhythm of So Hum is throwing you off, you may want to tack a few more minutes on.

tune up with tadasana

The worst time to go in for a checkup is when you're hacking up blood, just like the worst time to take your car in for a tune-up is right when the brakes stop working. Regular maintenance is key, which is why the best time to do Tadasana, a yoga posture designed to alleviate some of the stress and strain of day-to-day life, is probably right now.

① Stand up (if you aren't already) and place your feet hip-width apart, and turn the toes in slightly to keep the broadness of your lower back. Put a little more effort into your stance by creating "yoga feet," which just means engaging your feet a little more by spreading your toes into the mat.

2 Bring your weight a little more into your heels. Stand as sturdily as you can, feeling your leg muscles lengthen all the way up to your hips. Contract your quads—the goal is to create the strongest base possible so that your torso can stretch like a dang Slinky.

3 Place your hands on your hips and try to lift your torso in a way that creates length and space in the spine.

4 Bring your arms back to your sides without losing the lift of the spine, and lengthen up through the crown of your head. Try to balance your head over the pelvis so that you feel like a straight line of pure power.

5 Although this pose relies on tension, make sure you're comfortable. Take a few deep breaths in perfect alignment. Even when the rest of the world is askew, you have it together.

stop fucking around and get centered

You already know not to underestimate the physical impact of yoga—if you aren't careful, that shit can leave you sore for days. This exercise combines body scanning and Dirgha breathing to center you before a particularly intense bout of yoga. Go forth and stretch it out!

1 Sit in a comfortable, seated position with your legs crossed. Take a moment to let go of any obvious places of tension, especially in your neck, jaw, and eyes.

2 Keep scanning your way down your body, releasing tension where you find it, relaxing each body part, as you breathe in and out naturally.

3 After scanning the body, simply watch the breath as it flows in and out. Do this for a few breaths.

4 Begin Dirgha breathing. Remember Dirgha breathing? You want to feel the breath come in through your belly, ribs, and chest and then out the same way. We're talking deep, whalelike breaths.

5 Keep the Dirgha breathing going, especially if you noticed anything funky going on with your heart chakra specifically. This is your time to get everything in balance.

EXERCISE 62

loving your center

This simple exercise focuses on healing your physical center, otherwise known as your abdominal region, and doesn't even involve giving up dairy and gluten! Enjoy a big bowl of mac and cheese when you're done—it's officially on the mindfulness curriculum.

1. Stand on a yoga mat with your feet parallel, hip-width apart. Distribute your weight evenly between your feet and stand firm.

2. Lift the crown of your head toward the ceiling, stretching up like a majestic half giraffe, half human.

3. Take a deep breath in and float your arms up overhead with your palms turned in. Feel the stretch go all the way through the tips of your fingers.

4 Breathe out and fold at the hips, bending your knees just a little and sweeping your arms toward the floor. If you can't touch the floor with your hands, who fucking cares? As long as you're comfortable, you're killing it.

5 Stay balanced through the bend, putting some of your weight in your heels and raising your hips and butt toward the sky. If you can twerk, maybe throw a few celebratory shakes in there. If you hate fun, just keep breathing.

6 On an inhale, sweep back up to standing as you lengthen the front of your torso, reaching your arms up once again.

7 Repeat the movement five to ten times. Return to standing position and take a few chilled-out breaths.

make your throat chakra behave

The throat chakra handles all our communication, going beyond what we say out loud to all the other ways we express ourselves. If autocorrect is fucking you up and you keep spelling your name wrong when signing off emails, it's a sign that your throat chakra needs a refresher. Use some principles from Lion's Breath (back in Exercise 45) to clear things up.

1. Pose on all fours, on your hands and knees. In this position, do three rounds of Lion's Breath. Maybe it will be easier because you can pretend to be an actual lion? Remember to do a powerful exhalation with your tongue out and eyes rolled up. Return your face to normal, and repeat.

2. Change positions, sitting cross-legged with your hands in your lap.

3. Gently drop your chin down to your chest, and breathe seven deep breaths in this position, really feeling the air flow through your throat. Inhale again, and on the exhale gently roll your head to the right so that your right ear is near your right shoulder. Reverse the movement, rolling your head to the left on your next breath.

4. Bring your head back up in a neutral position and let yourself relax, looking out straight ahead of you. Your throat should be open and ready for declaring!

EXERCISE 64
literally just sitting

Sitting is the vanilla ice cream of these exercises, serving as the base for some premium toppings—the whipped cream that is sensory awareness, the cookie dough of mantra chanting, the Kahlúa shot of a good stretch. Sitting still with no adornment is an exercise in purely being present with yourself, within yourself. No matter what distractions arise, this is a position you can always return to.

1. If you're going to make a practice of just sitting, you're really going to want to sit still. Fidgeting is a slippery slope—move one finger and suddenly you're nailing the entirety of the "Single Ladies" choreography when you're supposed to be relaxing.

2. This exercise might be really hard, especially if you struggle with impulsiveness or chronic pain. Working through this discomfort and pain is a way to get to know yourself. Often when things are hard, it's because they have something to teach you. Start with five minutes at a time, and increase from there; work your way up to twenty minutes or as long as feels right.

get your subconscious to declutter

Even if you don't always feel like it, your body is an incredibly complex machine. Most of its systems and processes involve taking in one thing and getting rid of another: oxygen for carbon dioxide, energy for sweat, electrical impulses for movements, food for...well, you get it. Even on your laziest days, your body is hard at work getting rid of all the crap it doesn't need. Don't just thank your body, but also help it out with this hand mudra that encourages emotional, physical, and spiritual release.

1 Sit down in a comfortable meditation position. Hold your hands out so that the palms face up.

2 Curl the ring finger and middle finger of each hand to touch the fingertip of the thumb of the same hand.

3 Seriously, that's it! Hold this for a few minutes a couple of times a day and see how easily your body adapts to new things.

banish accordion body

You know how in old cartoons a piano will fall on someone and that person basically becomes a human accordion? That's what accumulated stress can feel like sometimes. In cartoon world, they solve this problem by inflating someone with air from a bicycle pump until the eyes bulge out of the person's head with an *awooga* noise, but luckily in the world of mindfulness, the solution is much, much simpler. This series of stretches is designed specifically to open up your body as a way to release tension.

1 Place a stool or armless chair next to the wall. Stand behind it with the left side of your body next to the wall.

2. Hoist your left foot up and place it on the stool or chair. You'll look like a Founding Father posing for a portrait. Glamour is glamour!

3. If you have trouble doing this comfortably, you can place a block or book under your right heel for a boost. Failing that, stilettos are always an option if you don't mind serious ankle injuries.

4. Inhale and lengthen the spine. Exhale and turn your body toward the wall, placing the fingertips of each hand on the wall at shoulder height but wider apart than the shoulders. Okay, now you look like you're posing for a nineties sad-girl-rock album cover. Are you sure you aren't a model?

5. Keep inhaling and lengthening. Yes, you're gorgeous and serving some serious poses, but openness is the point of this stretch, so unfortunately we have to prioritize it. Sigh. Breathe in, out, and so on.

6. After several breaths in this position, slowly unwind and release. Repeat on the other side of the body. Once you're all opened up, feel free to get your Top Model on however you want.

hey you?
stop it

Mindfulness is referred to as a "practice" not just because it makes it sound way fancier than "something you try for a few weeks and then ditch," but because no one, even total masters of it, are naturally great at it. Mindfulness is something you have to practice! On the plus side, unlike ice-skating or making the perfect guacamole, you can find a quick second to get better at mindfulness literally whenever. All you have to do is stop, breathe, and be.

1 You can do this whenever you have a free moment. Most meditation is about setting aside sacred time in your day to vibe, but this is something you can do whenever you need it. If you have trouble remembering, find ways to remind yourself: sticky notes, phone alarms, carrier pigeons.

2 Shut your eyes and take a moment to fully inhabit your body. Maybe don't do a super thorough body scan, but send little jolts of energy and awareness to the parts of your body that maybe aren't engaged or that have been working hard. For instance, if you've been at your desk typing all day, focus on your wrists and fingers.

3 As the awareness grows of the different parts of your body, use your breath to revitalize them. Inhale and send them good, uplifting energy. On the exhale, imagine you're releasing all the bad, gross, pent-up energy that's fucking your life up.

4 Take a few more breaths in and out, making adjustments to your body as needed so that you're totally comfortable. Make sure that being in your body feels relaxing, not terrible.

5 Return to real life by opening your eyes and taking a few seconds to express your gratitude for your brief moment of peace.

your chakras: live and in color!

If you still have trouble telling your root chakra from your third eye, use the rainbow to help you differentiate between them and keep them energized. Draw on the colors in your surroundings to bring some energy to any groggy chakras.

1 Your root chakra is usually depicted in red, so anything red is going to help deepen your connection to the earth—munch on an apple, apply a bold Marilyn Monroe lip, or buy some red roses to show your root chakra that you care.

2 The sacral chakra is orange, so sunrise and sunset are particularly powerful times for it. Whether you're a morning person or a night person, you can get some sweet orange light in your day and set your sacral chakra right.

3 Your solar plexus chakra is thought to be yellow, so all things sunny and bright will lead the way here. Squeeze a lemon on your salad, put on an old-school rain slicker, or just soak up some sun.

4 As if you needed another reason to believe that Valentine's Day is a scam, your heart chakra is green. Green! Strengthen your heart with a barefoot stroll in the grass, a leafy salad, a cup of matcha, or trying your hand at gardening.

5 Your throat chakra thrives off the color blue, so open up your lines of communication with some time by the ocean. If you're landlocked, don't despair! You have the whole sky at your disposal, so be sure to use a clear blue day to really connect with the people in your life.

6 The third eye chakra is indigo or purple, so the best time to really engage it is right as dusk falls and the sky turns purple. You can further energize it with some amethyst, lilacs, or, hell, grape soda probably works too.

7 True to its royal name, the crown chakra is usually white or gold. Golden hour isn't just an *Instagram* filter, but the time when your crown is ready to truly connect with the universe.

your dog knows something you don't

Whether taking cues from your dog's enthusiasm and gratitude for the presence of people or being inspired by your cat's commitment to breaking things for the hell of it, it turns out you can learn a lot from animals. Try seeing things from their point of view to connect with the world around you in a new way.

1 If you don't have a pet, watch some pups at a local park or just find some cute baby animal videos online. (Have you ever seen a baby sea lion learn to swim? It's better than Prozac.)

2 Focus on your surroundings. Are there trees around you? Buildings? How different might they look from an animal's eyes? What might be intimidating or exciting that is routine to you?

3 Engage your sense of hearing. No one is expecting you to somehow suddenly be able to hear dog whistles, but pay some attention to the subtle, quiet sounds in the distance. What's your response to them? How might you perceive them if you weren't yourself?

4 Bring your eyes to the ground, imagining it as your domain. How would the floor or the yard or the park seem if you were smaller? Would it feel like an endless expanse full of possibility or as cramped and crowded as it does right now? Is that why your dog goes absolutely apeshit at the dog park?

handle a big meal like a healthy adult

Okay, so the teachings of Ayurveda don't specifically say that this technique is best used after gorging on pie at Thanksgiving or getting carried away at Mexican restaurants with unlimited chips and salsa, but quite frankly, there's no better time to give your digestive system some encouragement.

1 First, drink a big glass of warm water. You can turn it into tea if you're so inclined, but if you're so full you can't move, plain warm water is fine.

2 Lie on your back with your legs straight out on the floor. If you're super full, you're probably already

doing this, so props to you for being a forward-thinking individual.

3 Take a few deep breaths, and relax into the support of the earth. No matter how big the food baby is, you're supported. Not even a twenty-piece chicken nugget combo meal can take that from you.

4 Bend your right knee and draw it up to your chest as far as is comfortable. Keep the left leg straight on the floor. Use both hands to hold the right knee into your chest. Breathe deeply several times, feeling your belly rise up against your right thigh.

5 On an exhale, straighten the right leg back onto the floor.

6 Repeat steps 4 and 5, using your other leg. You can do this for as long as is comfortable for you. It's really up to you!

7 Gently roll over onto your left side. Then, slowly get up.

speak your chakras' language

Because you can't physically see your chakras, you have to rely on other methods to really get a handle on them. You have already thought about using different colors, but there is another tool to add to your arsenal: sound. It turns out your chakras have pretty discerning taste, so when you DJ for them make sure to play what they like.

Simply choose the chakra you want to affect and chant the sound that is associated with it:

- O as in OM or OMG for the root

- OO as in POOL or OOPS, DID I FUCK THIS UP ALREADY for the sacral

- AH as in DHARMA or HAHA, I'M LITERALLY TALKING TO MY CHAKRAS for the solar plexus

- A as in SPACE or BABIES MAKE THESE SOUNDS for the heart

- E as in FREE or THREE MORE CHAKRAS TO GO for the throat

- MM as in MEDIUM or MAYBE I SHOULD KEEP THE VOLUME DOWN; MY ROOMMATE IS BANGING ON THE WALL for the third eye

- ING as in WING or THIS THING BETTER WORK OR I'M GOING TO LOSE MY SHIT for the crown

Chant the appropriate sound while sitting calmly, being mindful of your breathing, and concentrating on the sound and on feeling it surge through the associated chakra.

record your reiki triumphs

Yes, you'll need a literal physical journal—we're going retro for this one. Why? The physical act of writing, even for just a few quick sentences, allows for greater freedom of expression than a computer or your Notes app might.

1. Open the notebook with a few pages (or paragraphs, hell, even sentences) about where you are right now and why the concept of Reiki is of interest to you. You'll return to this entry as you progress through your journey, so try to be honest and specific.

2. Every day you do Reiki, no matter how little or simple the effort is, log it in your notebook. You can be as straightforward or as rambling as you like. This is a private space for you to explore a deeply internal process. Also, you can curse as much as you want. Shit! Fuck! Bitch! Ass!

3. You can also use this notebook to record your intentions, since they'll influence your Reiki practice. Also, you may appreciate being able to look back at them and see how much your goals have or haven't changed.

oil massage for one:
not as sad as it sounds

If you're an insomniac or just want to pamper yourself, an Ayurveda-influenced foot massage is a great way to unwind.

1. Different oils work for different doshas. In general, vata and kapha types tend to respond well to sesame oil, and pitta types tend to like coconut oil, though obviously personal preferences and sensitivities come into play here.

2. Heat up the oil until it's warm to the touch—you aren't trying to deep-fry yourself, so gentle, light heat is best.

3. Begin by massaging your feet and thanking them for carrying you all day. Let's face it: Feet aren't the prettiest part of your body, but every dog has its day.

4. Wash your hands and put on socks. It may feel a little weird to sleep with socks on, but would you rather have cozy sock feet or oily sheets? Thought so.

warrior pose: be a bad bitch!

Some yoga is all about calming you down. Not warrior pose. This is an invigorating position that makes you feel ready to conquer your nemeses, even if it's just Diane from accounting.

1. Stand with your arms by your sides and your legs together. Start off with a bang by jumping or walking your legs four feet apart. Extend your arms to the sides, palms facing up, and take a deep breath as you lift them over your head. Be as dynamic as you can in every movement.

2. Lengthen your arms farther, making the shape of a V. Your elbows are going to try to disobey you by bending, but don't give in. You're a warrior! If you give in to your elbows, what's next? Actually reading Diane's emails? Fuck no.

3. Turn your left foot in (forty-five to sixty degrees) and revolve your right leg out. Exhale and turn your body to face your right (front) leg. Next, lift your entire body off the ground, starting from the arches of your feet. Ground through your feet, lift the arches, and extend all the way from your feet to your legs, the side body, and your fingertips. Try to keep your expression soft. Diane must think you come in peace.

4. Take another big breath in, and bend your right leg on the exhale so that your knee is over your ankle.

5. If you can, find some more length in your left leg all the way from your hip to your heel, and bend your right leg so that it creates a right angle. You should be finding flexibility that you didn't know you had. Admire it and stay in the pose for a few breaths.

6. When you feel charged up with power, exit the pose by pressing your feet back into the floor and straightening out your front leg. Slowly shift your feet back to parallel position, and face center once more. Jump your legs back together.

7. Repeat on the other side. Once Diane's next email enters your inbox, your inner warrior is going to throw a "per my last email" at her so hard she won't know what hit her. Now *that's* power.

realize your life isn't boring

There's nothing wrong with your days being similar—getting up, going to work, and going back home with a few meals in between is a perfectly reasonable way to live your life! What keeps a routine life feeling full and fresh is regularly taking stock of the moments that made each day special. Run through this list of questions at the end of the day and see what jumps out at you.

1 What did I do right after I woke up this morning and how did I feel? Did I realize I had five extra minutes to sleep? Did I feel weird because I had that eerily realistic dream about being a lizard? Did I immediately check my phone and get irrationally mad that no one texted me between the

hours of 11 p.m. and 7 a.m. on a Wednesday? Do I not matter or something? Jeez!

2 Was I rushing around this morning, running late, or wondering how I'd be able to squeeze everything into the day? Did I have to go back home twice because I thought I forgot my keys and my wallet only to realize that I had them the whole time?

3 What did I eat today? How did I feel after I ate it? Did I give myself time to enjoy it, or did I eat it hunched over at my desk?

4 Did I find time for myself, to take a pause, breathe, or laugh? Did I enjoy getting into a spirited debate with my coworkers about the best kind of french fry? Was it refreshing for me to drink a glass of wine and eat cereal for dinner, or was it, in retrospect, the bad kind of crazy?

5 How am I feeling right now? What do I have to look forward to tomorrow?

how not to cry in public

Listen, if you're in a state of heightened emotion, you can't just *breathe* your way out of it. If that was true the whole world would be run by happy, well-adjusted people who happen to pant like dogs for sixteen hours a day. What this kind of breathing can help with is that pinch you get behind your eyes when you're pretending you aren't upset in public, whether you're at work or getting dumped on what you thought was going to be an awesome date.

1 Go outside, if possible. If you can't, escaping from the scene of tension or anxiety in any way you can is recommended. When you're in a place with shitty vibes, it's going to be that much harder to control your emotions.

2 As always, begin by paying attention to your breath. If you're breathing hard or irregularly, try to focus on soft, gentle inhalations and exhalations. You want to really feel them expanding in your chest and belly.

3 Find a mantra or phrase that gives you some comfort that you can repeat in your head. If you're somewhere secluded, say it out loud. It can be "I am safe here," or "I will be okay," or even "This sucks shit but it won't kill me." If it helps, use it.

4 Find a rhythm where the words and the breaths intertwine. Settle into it for a few moments, breathing and repeating.

5 Once you feel more in control, assess how you feel. If you still want to cry after getting in touch with your inner self, who are you to argue? Shed some tears and get back to business.

"I am safe here..."

EXERCISE 77

stand up, dummy

When walking meditation feels passé and the idea of sitting makes you want to jump out a window, don't despair. Split the difference with standing meditation for a quick burst of mindfulness.

1 Stand with your feet parallel, hip-width apart.

2 Stand tall with your arms by the sides, shoulders relaxed.

3 Do a quick check for resting bitch face. Chances are, if you're meditating during the workday it's because you're *pissed*. Take a sec to relax the muscles in your face, shoulders, and jaw.

4 Begin breathing through your nose, using your nostrils for both the inhalation and exhalation. Your

mouth is not invited to this standing party right now! It's standing at the door while a bouncer keeps telling it that the club is too full. Pay it no mind. Keep breathing through your nose.

5. With your feet hip-width apart, turn your toes in and heels out just a bit so your feet are slightly pigeon-toed.

6. Exhale and bend your knees slightly. You should feel a shift as gravity moves your weight down into your heels. Make gravity's life a little easier by really letting your feet sink into the ground.

7. Although your feet are sturdy, try to relax any tension from your knees up. You want to feel like you're using as little muscle as possible.

8. Keep your gaze steady and soft as you sink even deeper into this pose. You should be feeling supported by your bones alone, no muscles needed.

9. To release, bring your feet back to parallel, inhale, and sweep your arms to the sides and overhead as your legs straighten. Press your palms together and exhale, while bringing them down to prayer position at the heart. Take a final deep breath, and then exit the stance fully.

pimp my mind(fulness)

Most mindfulness exercises follow pretty much the same structure, going from awareness of the physical world to the physical body and then finally to the mind. This is the most bare-bones version of mindfulness that you can customize to your needs however you want. Do it at the gym so you can do a workout perfect for what your body needs. Do it while scrolling through *Netflix* to find a show that fits your particular mood. Shit, use it to customize a burrito bowl. The sky's the limit.

1. Always start with "scanning" or "sweeping" your body from bottom to top. Start with your feet; move up in sequence to your calves, thighs, torso, arms, neck, and head. This can be as quick or intensive as your heart desires—if you want to go through the state of each of your toe knuckles individually, that's up to you. Let freedom ring!

2. Next, focus on how your surroundings are interacting with your body. Is the air cold or hot? Are you sitting somewhere comfortable, or are you hiding in the bathroom at a party you didn't want to go to?

3. You know what's next: Check in with your breathing. You really can't do it enough! The purpose of this exercise is to just be aware of *how* you're breathing, not to do it according to any prescribed pattern. Just acknowledge what you're working with for now.

4. Once you've taken stock of yourself and your surroundings, add a few more exercises that will get you more relaxed. If you're feeling disconnected from your body, try some stretches to re-engage with it. If you're tense, focus on breathing to release that tension. Try to follow your intuition here.

stop worrying about murderers and go to sleep

What do you think about before you fall asleep? The time in third grade you called your teacher "mom"? Whether the creak you thought you just heard is a knife-wielding murderer or just your cat? Everyone's thoughts go to some weird places before bed (which is to say nothing of how fucked up your dreams can get), but you can at least try to guide them in the right direction with some visualization.

1. Get comfortable, and close your eyes.

2. Take stock of your own comfort. Maybe you've settled into that spot on the mattress that's shaped exactly like your body, or your ratty old pajama shirt is feeling particularly soft today. Whatever makes you feel good, appreciate it.

3. If you really, really can't sleep, try to imagine your absolute dream bed. Maybe you'll imagine a massive four-poster bed in a castle with a roaring fire in the corner, or a cozy bunk in a rustic log cabin with the sounds of nature lulling you to sleep. Try to place yourself there as vividly as possible, focusing on sights, sounds, smells, and whatever else you can come up with. As long as it's soothing, it belongs in your fantasy.

4. If all else fails, add more detail, like, what kind of crown molding is in the room or what zoning codes your space abides by. If you can't fantasize yourself into sleeping, maybe you can bore yourself into it?

EXERCISE 80

force a friend into yoga

If some of your mindfulness practices leave your friends and family giving you the side-eye (you mean not *everyone* is obsessed with their breathing?), dare them to give it a try themselves. Partnered yoga is the most low-key way to introduce someone to the benefits of yoga, combining all the great shit you know and love about yoga with the added self-care benefit of giving your communication skills a workout too.

1 Stand with your partner shoulder to shoulder, facing the same direction, holding hands, with your inside feet touching. Yes, hold hands! Partner yoga is also a powerful tool in your flirting arsenal. Just know that your stance shouldn't be the only thing matching; you guys should have similar intentions and energy too. Otherwise, things will get weird fast.

2 Each take a big step to the side with the outer foot, turning that foot out ninety degrees.

3 With a good, strong hold, bend your outer leg so your knee is positioned above your middle toe. Lift the outside arm to shoulder height and reach in the same direction as your foot. Rotate your head to look over your outstretched hand. You may end up face-to-face with your partner or face-to-butt with your partner, depending on how you both turn. Treat both face and ass with the same respect.

4 Check in with your partner. Remember that bodies are weird as fuck and everyone has their own limits, so be nice. Even if you have a very funny joke about your partner's weird toes on deck, hold it in.

5 Hold for three or four breaths. Encourage each other to see what else you can do in the pose, sinking deeper or stretching further to *really* feel it.

6 Let the other person know when you're ready to exit the pose. Try to align the way you change positions.

7 Thank your partner, maybe tucking a piece of hair behind your ear shyly if you really want to make it feel like a rom-com. Then get back to yoga-ing by repeating on the other side.

keep your presence in the present

Anxiety has a way of making everything feel urgent, but if you look a little closer, you'll notice that a vast majority of anxious feelings don't actually focus on what's in front of you! Instead of actually being a useful response to the stimuli you're facing, anxiety decides to obsess over whether that thing you said three years ago was weird, or all the medieval diseases you might come down with in the future. What the fuck is up with that? When fear is taking you out of the present, use your chakras to remind yourself where and when you are and that you, not anxiety, are the one running the show.

1. Sit down with as much awareness as you can of the placement of your body.

2. Touch the base of your spine, where your root chakra hooks into your body, and visualize it glowing bright red. Focus as much attention and presence as you can on this specific spot.

3. Move your hands to your lower abdomen to get in touch with your sacral chakra. Focus on the color orange, and pay special attention to the way breath expands and contracts.

4. Shift your focus and hands slightly upward to rest on your solar plexus. If you notice your mind jumping back to your anxieties, remind yourself that those thoughts don't belong to this moment. What the fuck can you do about a past that's already happened or a future that you can't predict? Exactly.

5. Continue this up your body at the heart, throat, and third eye chakras.

6. Finally, place your hands on top of your head at the crown. Through your hands, visualize calming, healing white light flooding your brain through this chakra. Stay with this light for as long as you need, remaining in the present as best you can.

sometimes self-care sucks

Self-care doesn't always look like doing whatever you want to do whenever you want to do it. If that was the case, most of us would never get anything done beyond stress baking and marathon napping. Sometimes self-care is doing the thing that's good for you even if you're dreading it. If you need a boost to gear up for something that might be unpleasant but will pay off in the end, keep this handy little exercise on deck.

1 Sit in a comfortable position for meditation, with your sitting bones firmly planted on the chair, or on a cushion if you are on the floor. Since you're gearing up for a challenge, the least you can do is be comfortable, dammit! Find a good balance for your posture between natural and upright.

2. Relax your jaw and all the muscles of your face. Do a brief body scan, relaxing every single muscle along the way. Little ones like your fingers should get the same treatment as your abs and quads. No one gets left behind here.

3. In your new, relaxed state, take a few natural-feeling breaths. Appreciate just how dang good it feels to breathe with as little tension in your body as possible.

4. Take your self-scan one step deeper with a chakra scan. Shut your eyes and starting at your crown chakra, visualize the color of each chakra as you move down your body. Hold each color in your mind for a few breaths.

5. Once you reach your root chakra, take a few breaths with a clear mind. No more scanning or visualizing, just breathing purely for yourself.

6. Place both of your hands over your heart in prayer position with the side of your hands touching. For the last few breaths, listen to your heartbeat as you exit the meditation ready to conquer whatever the fuck the world has in store.

you're a crystal mofo now

Something about crystals is just so goddamn satisfying. While you can fuck up yoga by falling over and meditation by thinking, there's no wrong way to own a crystal. Even if you decide after all is said and done that crystals are bullshit, they're still pretty and look nice on a shelf! You also really can't go wrong by adding a crystal to meditation or manifestation exercises. You really can use any crystal you're drawn to, but quartz and amethyst tend to be easiest to find in stores and affordable to boot.

1. If your crystal is brand new, leave it for a few days in a spot where it can absorb some sunlight and, for the witchy ones out there, moonlight. Keep the crystal near you, but not in your hands just yet.

2 Take a moment to bring to mind one big thing that your heart desires. Be loud enough so you can drown out all the dumb obstacles that fear and reality just love to shove in your face.

3 Hell yeah, it's crystal time! With the image still in your head, pick up the crystal, and hold it inside your cupped hands: one hand on top of the other, with the crystal inside.

4 Feel the energy of the crystal. Remember, you charged that shit in sunlight *and* moonlight! It's pulsing with powerful cosmic energy, so let it flow. If you can't bring yourself to accept the idea of a rock having energy, that's okay too. Just enjoy the weight of it in your hands.

friendly fucking reminder: charge your crystals, charge your phone

Skeptics might find the practice of charging a crystal to be, frankly, kind of insane. Maybe it is! But in the world of crystal collectors and fanatics, giving your crystal some time in the sunlight and moonlight is a way to infuse it with the earthly and cosmic energy it needs to really live its best little crystal life.

let it go

You may be over *Frozen* but you have to admit: Elsa had a point. Sometimes the best way through a problem isn't meditation or deep breathing but just throwing it in the trash. Use the power of visualization to make like a true ice queen and let that shit go.

1. Sit or lie in a position for meditation and breathe in and out comfortably.

2. Bring the issue or thought troubling you to the forefront of your mind. Listen to it without judgment, remembering that it's taking up so much space in your mind because it has something to say to you.

3. There's a few different ways to make these thoughts quiet down. Try imagining the thought as a little cartoon fly and trapping it in a jar. Hear its voice getting quieter and quieter as you tighten the lid. Calm down, you aren't suffocating it, just quieting it. Also, it's literally in your imagination.

4 Envision these thoughts as balloons, except instead of crying when you let one go into the atmosphere, you're overjoyed. If you want to jazz things up you can even imagine them bursting or getting sucked into an airplane engine.

5 Use your imagination and don't feel like you're just ignoring problems! Real estate in your brain is expensive, dammit, so make sure that the right crowd is living there!

make anxiety useful for once

Anxiety is a total fucking jerk. You'll be going about your business and then, bam, all of a sudden you're on the floor because your brain just won't *shut up*. Anxiety, even though it can be felt throughout the body, is caused by a fuckton of energy in your brain, and chakra healing has a pretty brilliant way to deal with this imbalance: Just send the energy down. *Way* down. Yes, we're talking about the root chakra. While it might be located in a particularly unglamorous place, its grounding effects are just what you need to let that anxious energy dissipate. If you aren't ready to go all in with chakras just yet, you can also use this as a more general grounding exercise to get you out of your head and back into your body.

1. If the weather permits, get outside! The root chakra draws majorly on the energy of the earth, so the closer you can get to the action, the better.

2. Sit or stand in a sturdy position, with your feet firmly on the ground. Plant your hands somewhere, too, if you can—fidgety hands are one of anxiety's closest allies. Feel the sturdiness of the surface below you, and try to draw some comfort from it. No matter what bullshit is happening in your head, the ground ain't moving.

3. Take deep, centered breaths. It might be hard if you're really going through it, but try your hardest to place your attention on breathing instead of fear. Let each breath you take flow all the way through to the ground.

4. For several minutes, breathe and envision energy coming down into the body and flowing into the earth. Anxiety can make you feel weak, but if you can take your mind off your anxiety and onto your breathing for just a few seconds, congratulate yourself. Your brain is a badass, and so are you.

EXERCISE 86
pranayama with anuloma viloma

You're probably sick of the word "breathing" by now, which is why this exercise is called "Pranayama with Anuloma Viloma" and not "Breathing Deluxe." This exercise is designed to center you and can be used anytime when you're feeling particularly riled.

1 Sit in a comfortable seated position.

2 Warm up with Nadi Shodhana, aka alternate nostril breathing. Drawing a blank? Flip to Exercise 12.

3 With each deep breath you take, pause for a few seconds between the completion of your inhale and beginning of your exhale. Start with just a second or so as you get comfortable with it.

4 As you adapt to the break between inhaling and exhaling, see if you can hold your breath a little longer. Don't feel like you're depriving yourself of air; after all, you're in total control here!

5 Repeat for up to fifteen minutes.

say it loud and proud

Maybe you're getting better at declaring your wants during manifestation sessions but still can't give a straight answer when your friend asks where you want to go for dinner. Take a day to be as declarative as you can about what you want—try this:

1. Make your request reasonable. You don't want to be pulling shit like asking your friend to give you $500 on Venmo. What's wrong with you?

2. Don't give a bunch of reasons why your friend should comply. You're not necessarily looking to convince people, just to declare your intention to the people around you. Besides, no one is listening when you go off on a tangent like that anyway.

3. Be firm, but don't sulk if you don't get your way.

4. Don't lose track with the needs of people around you! Declaring your intention and owning your needs is great, but if your friend or partner looks like they've had a shitty day, maybe reconsider.

5. Be nice, dammit! No one, including the universe, likes to see a total dick get what they want.

caffeinate and mean it

Mindfulness is a beautiful enough thing on its own, but when you combine it with caffeine, well, you're onto something really, really good. While using powdered or loose tea is the traditional choice for this ritual, making pour-over coffee or using a hand-powered espresso contraption would probably also do if you're craving a more caffeine-heavy mindful moment.

1 Prepare your heat source.

2 Pour the water slowly and deliberately into the kettle. While normally you might just dump it into the pot, remember that you're trying to notice and appreciate things you'd just ignore in your quest to fuel your espresso addiction. So when the water flows into the pot, really watch it!

3 Watch the water as it heats. Observe it as you wait for it to reach a rolling boil. Turn off the heat and add the tea. Cover it and let it steep.

4 Strain the tea and pour it into a cup. Remember, keep moving slowly and keep your focus on the little moments of the process.

5 Pick up the cup with your right hand and place it in the left hand, with the fingers of the right hand still around the cup. Make a small, polite bow. Even if no one is around, take it as your chance to celebrate all the waiting and watching you just did.

6 Let the scent of your tea waft to your nose and really take in the smell.

7 Drink your tea in small sips. You can add milk, sugar, or lemon if you want, but at least give yourself a chance to really experience the undiluted flavor of the tea at first. Use your sense of taste to pick up on the full breadth of the flavor.

8 When you're finished, take a deep breath. Then turn the cup counterclockwise ninety degrees with your thumb and forefinger back to its original position when you picked it up. Voila, caffeine and mindfulness in one!

trick your sense of balance

Did you know that just standing with your hands on your hips and repeating the phrase "I'm so excited" can increase your confidence, despite looking absolutely idiotic? Our physical behavior influences our brains way more than we realize, and we're a lot less complex than we think we are. This applies doubly to the relentless pursuit of mental balance in adult life! People sweat and fret aiming for a balance they never seem to achieve, so see if a basic balancing exercise is enough to trick your brain into thinking you have it all figured out.

1. Stand upright, feet slightly spaced, with your dominant foot about four inches in front of the other. Balance yourself in this position. Take some deep breaths in this balanced position.

2. That first step was too easy to be the whole thing—you should know that by now! You're going to bend your knees slightly and start to rock, forward and back. Keep it slow and deliberate, like you're skateboarding or surfing. Hang ten, my dudes.

3. Keep rocking and shifting your balance for a few minutes, slowing down the pace until you come to a standstill. Switch over so your other foot is in the front and repeat on the other side.

4. Notice what impacts your balance the most. Learn to anticipate the challenges to your balance and work through them. See if you can apply this to the other things that might throw you off during the day.

take purification breaths

If you ever feel at a distance from your normal self, try Buddhism's purifications of the soul. Focusing on the elements of earth, water, fire, and air, it's a simple way to get back in touch with your body's natural state.

1 Buddhist practice usually mandates doing this in the morning since that's when these elements are at their peak. Between us, 11 a.m. has just as much earth, air, water, and fire as 4 a.m.

2 First, you'll connect with the earth. You can do this by looking out the window, standing in your yard, caring for your houseplant—as long as you feel one

with the dirt. Once you feel in touch with the planet, take a deep breath through your nose. Visualize a stream of energy going straight from the ground through your nose and fanning out through your body. Repeat this four times for a total of five breaths.

3. The next set of breaths is all about water. Imagine the movement and energy of water in whatever way you like. With your next breath, imagine a stream of water entering your nose and trickling down your throat, rushing out to your spine and crown to wash away whatever you don't want. Negativity, frustration, the urge to look at an ex's *Instagram*—let the water sweep it away. Do five sets of these breaths.

4. Fire is the focus of this next set of breaths, with a special focus on using the heat and power to pump up your heart chakra. Catch some rays from the sun or light a candle, and breathe slowly and deeply. Let the breath flow to your crown and heart. Exhale through your nose, you dragon!

5. Lastly is air-focused breath. Take a deep inhalation, appreciating the fact that air is all around you. It doesn't just enter through your nose, but also through every pore on your body. After five sets of this, your breathing will be whipped into shape.

do a standing wide-angle forward fold

This pose is the yoga equivalent of flopping onto your couch after an especially irritating day. If you aren't someone who can touch your toes, feel free to give your knees a little bend while doing this; otherwise, congrats on acing the Presidential Physical Fitness Test back in fifth grade, show-off.

1 Stand with your feet three to four feet apart with hands on your hips.

2 Take some time to adjust your stance. Make sure your feet are parallel with each other and pressed firmly into the floor. Keep the strength going

through your legs. You want a super strong base to get the benefits of this pose, so try not to half-ass it.

3 Take a deep, cleansing breath in. We're talking the kind of breath that lifts your chest up. Raise your arms with it. While lifting your arms isn't technically part of the position as traditionalists do it, it's so much more dramatic and satisfying.

4 Fold yourself forward, making sure you hinge at your hips. You don't want to go all the way down just yet, so for the first part of the fold, make sure your torso is parallel to the floor.

5 Now, keep bending forward like you're going to touch the floor. If you can do it, touch the floor and ground yourself with both your hands and feet. If you can't, use yoga blocks or give your knees a slight bend. It isn't cheating—it's *modifying*.

6 Try to find a little more length in your arms and legs, giving your excess energy and feelings some space to swirl around and work themselves out.

7 Gaze straight down, and take five to ten deep breaths.

dance like a dumbass

With all respect to Buddha and friends, sometimes stillness just doesn't cut it. An impromptu dance party for one is a remedy for just about anything—whatever you're dealing with, let some mood-appropriate music take the wheel. The phrase "dance like nobody's watching" may make you want to hurl, but embrace it in all its corny glory. Here's what to do:

1. Put on clothes that make you want to move! Maybe its sweatpants, maybe it's more appropriate for the club, but as long as it makes you want to prance and dance, it's all good.

2. If you are self-conscious, close the curtain/shades. Actually, even if you aren't self-conscious, this might be a good idea.

3 Choose your music based on your mood. Feeling angry and want to get it all out? Go for some heavy metal. Looking for a mood boost? Put on something with a fast beat. Up for a challenge? Throw on some whale sounds and get your interpretive dance on.

4 Play your music loud and dance! Don't worry about being good or giving off a certain vibe while you dance. This is all about connecting with the music and trusting your body to move. Whether your body wants to crawl on the floor like a modern dance major or drop it low like J.Lo, you're doing it right.

5 When you're done, drink some water and take some time to thank your body for its sweet moves.

don't fill the space with bullshit

If you say "wow, that's crazy" as a conversational space filler more than three times a day, try a day of silence. Obviously, you won't be able to be 100 percent quiet, so for the times you have no choice but to talk, really be mindful about the words you use—you'll find that restricting the amount you talk makes the things you do say matter more. What the hell can you do if you're staying silent for a whole day? Try one of these ideas:

- **Read a book.** Let's be honest: You probably have a shelf of books you've been meaning to read "when you have time." Well, bitch, this is it. Plus, nothing takes your mind off your own life like getting involved in a good story.

- **Journaling.** Not only is this good to get some of your genius thoughts down, but it's also great when you are batshit mad and need to get your frustrations out without yelling.

- **Listen to music/podcasts.** Just because you're not talking doesn't mean you can't listen to your favorite artists sing or speak their truths.

- **Write a letter.** Or if you can't be bothered with that, try an email, or, if you are super lazy, a text.

- **Meditate.** Hello! The ultimate way to relax and feel calmer is meditation. Plus most meditations are silent, so you don't have to change what you're doing anyway!

love your body at your own pace

Self-love is hard, so pursue it in small steps. Just say thank you to your body whenever you can. Are you having a good hair day? Thank your mane. Walking a few miles? Give your feet some props. Here are some things to do to feel better about the skin you are in:

- **Focus on your health.** If you are healthy, that's really what matters. If you are breathing and feeling well, then you are already winning! Whenever your body is doing what it needs to do to keep you going, that is cause for celebration.

- **Eat what you want because food is fucking delicious.** Studies have shown that people who don't deprive themselves and eat what they want in moderation have fewer weight issues. Try to eat things that make you feel good, both physically and mentally. Sometimes it'll be a huge green salad full of seasonal veggies, other times, well, you just gotta bring on the off-brand cheese puffs.

- **Look in the mirror.** It's been proven that speaking positively to yourself can grow your self-love. So look in your eyes and tell yourself, "I love you." Sure you may feel like a whack-a-do, but if it helps improve your body image and doesn't involve sit-ups, it's worth it!

I love you.

work with your hands

One of the reasons people today feel so drawn to mindfulness is because there's just so much shit competing for their attention. When was the last time you watched a movie without juggling *Instagram*, emails, and googling the plot of the movie you're watching? Take up a hobby that occupies multiple senses—needlepoint! drawing! ukulele! origami!—not only are they meditative and stress reducing on their own, but they'll also build your ability to remain focused on just one thing at a time.

Working with your hands also helps you:

- **Build your confidence:** When you take on a project with your hands, say knitting, you have to make many small decisions about what to do in the process. What color yarn do I use? Do I know any babies who need to wear cute little hats? Does this look good or am I insane? Projects that encourage decisiveness help you build confidence when it comes to making big choices down the line.

- **Gain self-awareness:** Life is busy and noisy, and a lot of your thoughts get lost in the shuffle, but when you work creatively with your hands, you get to express yourself in a whole new way without letting any noise get in the way. Maybe you'll learn something new about yourself, like you're fucking awesome at drawing or have a knack for tricky pastry recipes. Anything that lets you surprise yourself is a good use of your time.

- **Find peace:** Working with your hands puts you in a kind of meditative state as you focus just on what your hands are doing. Try to treat it the way you'd treat any other kind of meditation. Set aside time to work on your hobby, uninterrupted and without background noise. If you really have trouble with classic silent meditation, who knows? Maybe this will take its place! This helps you feel calm and less stressed.

be unavailable—for real

While most of these exercises aren't designed to interrupt the flow of your life, remember that there is a nuclear option you can deploy if you need to. Pick one day to spend with yourself and shut your phone off. No calls, texts, emails, alerts, alarms, nothing.

Don't post that moment/meal/achievement on social media; instead, just enjoy it for yourself.

Don't respond to that text. Let it linger unanswered. You can do that shit later. It can wait.

Watch your inbox fill up and don't open your email; most of those issues will sort themselves out without you. Maybe take a personal day to avoid any unfair accusations of slacking. You aren't "shirking responsibility"; you're "living mindfully" so suck on that, rude bosses of the world!

Leave your phone at home and go for a walk. Maybe take a route you're familiar with, just to be on the safe side. Getting lost without your GPS is a surefire way to fuck up your day of blissful unavailability.

Just live one day on your own schedule—you'll be amazed how great that shit feels.

EXERCISE 97
burn it

Stop salivating, pyros; you aren't going to light just anything on fire. If there's something you really can't let go of, try writing it down and then lighting the paper on fire. Here's what to do:

1. First, you'll need paper, a pen, matches or a lighter, and a fire-friendly receptacle (glass or metal bowl, fireplace, firepit, and so on).

2. Make sure you are feeling calm and centered. If you're not try one of the calming meditations in this book. You do not want to be some crazy wacko lighting a bonfire out of spite.

3. Write down on the paper, in as much detail as you can, what you want to let go of.

4. Now light the paper on fire and place it in your fire-friendly receptacle. Watch it burn, take a few deep breaths, and feel your attachment to whatever that shit was leave your body.

5. That's it. You're free of that crappy thing and you can move into your future without it.

flip the jealousy switch and be nice

The world we live in is designed to produce envy, and a dangerous flip side to the Law of Attraction is jealousy, especially when someone has the thing you really, really want, to the point where you think about wanting it multiple times a day. When this happens, don't resent or make judgments out of envy. Take a *metta* moment and wish them well, asking the universe to keep caring for them. Here's a simple way to let jealousy go:

1. Focus on something you find beautiful or desirable. It could be in a shop window, in a museum, something you see on another person on the street—it can be anything.

2. Next, stop and admire the object for five minutes. Feel your feeling of desire or longing grow. Want it with every fiber of your being. Let your mind get a little crazy thinking about just how your life would change if you had this thing.

3. Now let it go. Walk away, turn around, leave the room, do a visualization of it floating away, whatever you need to do to abruptly let it go.

4. You let that shit go! See how it feels to admire something and want it but to be able to continue on without it? The best part is that nothing was actually taken away from you! You still have all the amazing shit you had before, *plus* the badass ability to let go.

get rid of
the bad lies

Lying isn't always bad! If you're having a shitty day but say, "Oh, same old, same old," instead of "I'm dying inside," when your coworker asks you how it's going, well, that's just social decency. But lying to your loved ones at the expense of your own feelings? Hell no. Keep a tally of all the little white lies you tell during the day that mask your own emotions and try to pursue honesty, starting with the things you tell yourself. Sometimes we lie to avoid revealing things about ourselves that we don't like. A good way to be honest with yourself is to heal your throat chakra.

Give this a try:

1. Sit in a comfortable position with your eyes closed.

2. Breathe and concentrate on bringing energy up through the root chakra, sacral chakra, solar plexus chakra, heart chakra, and finally up to your throat.

3. With each deep inhale, imagine a blue light glowing around your throat getting bigger and bigger.

4. Think about getting rid of all the negative shit that is blocking your throat and replacing it with this blue light. You may feel your throat loosening up as you do this and you might even burp. Let it out buddy. You're safe here.

5. Continue breathing in this light until you feel relaxed and your throat feels open.

Now go forth and tell the truth; stop weighing yourself down with those nasty lies.

hug three people
(with consent)

Physical touch is an incredibly powerful force, which is why it matters that you get permission before doing this. There will be none of this "I'm a hugger" bullshit where you hug now, ask questions later. On days you're feeling disconnected from humanity, see if you can find three living things to hug—friends, family members, or a pet. The point here is to be mindful and aware of the moment of the hug. Here's how:

1. Stand facing your hug partner and take in a few deep breaths. Be in the present moment and try not to let your thoughts drift away.

2. Smile at your partner and then take him or her in your arms.

3. Hug the person with all your heart and spirit. Really put your whole self into it. Appreciate this person and all that he or she is to you.

4. Release your partner; you don't want to be that clinger who doesn't know when to let go.

index